Walter Gresham House
(The Bishop's Palace)
1887–92

Trueheart-Adriance Building
1881

HISTORIC GALVESTON

PHOTOGRAPHED BY RICHARD PAYNE
WRITTEN BY GEOFFREY LEAVENWORTH
FOREWORD BY CYNTHIA MITCHELL
EDITED BY STEPHEN BARNHILL
GALVESTON CHRONOLOGY BY MARY REMMERS
DESIGNED BY JERRY HERRING
PRODUCED BY JERRY HERRING AND DANCIE PERUGINI WARE
PUBLISHED BY HERRING PRESS, HOUSTON

HP 85

Hendley Row
1855–59

ACKNOWLEDGMENTS

Many people contributed to the creation of this book. Indeed, *Historic Galveston* was a collaborative effort. We wish first to thank George and Cynthia Mitchell, whose support of the project was invaluable. We are grateful to the archivists and research librarians of Rosenberg Library and the Galveston and Texas History Center, especially Jane Kenamore, Uli Haller, and Casey Greene; to Betty Hartman, Virginia Eisenhour, and Margaret Swett Henson for their prior works; to Gwen Marcus and Peter Brink of the Galveston Historical Foundation, and to Mary Remmers. We want also to thank Etta Brashear and Bob Nesbitt for their work. Finally, we owe a special debt to our administrative assistants, Jane MacFarlane, Ann Nava, Vicki Yates, Anne Magner, and, even more to Sandy Herring, Jim Ware, Suzanne Byrd, Simone Leavenworth, and Karen Barnhill.

J.H., D.P.W., R.P., G.L., S.B.

Houston, Texas
February 15, 1985

THIS BOOK
IS ENDORSED BY
THE GALVESTON HISTORICAL
FOUNDATION

Published by
Herring Press, Inc.
1216 Hawthorne
Houston, Texas 77006
(713) 526-1250

Distributed by
Texas Monthly Press
P.O. Box 1569
Austin, Texas 78767
(512) 476-7085

Typesetting by
Professional Typographers

Printed in Japan by
Dai Nippon

Library of Congress
Catalog Card Number 85-80070

ISBN 0-917001-02-8

RICHARD PAYNE
Photographer

Richard Payne, a native of Paris, Texas, studied photography in Germany in the 1950s before returning to his home state to graduate from Texas Tech University in 1960 with a degree in architecture. He became a registered architect in Texas in 1974, and then combined his two professional interests when he formed Richard Payne Architect/ Photographer in 1968. Since that time, Richard's photographs have appeared in the major architectural publications of the United States, England, Japan, and Germany, and in a 1979 volume, *Johnson/Burgee: Architecture.*

GEOFFREY LEAVENWORTH
Writer

Geoffrey Leavenworth, whose writing has appeared in the *New York Times, Discover, Money,* the *Christian Science Monitor, Harper's Bazaar,* and many other publications, has been a resident of Galveston Island since 1981. A 1975 graduate of the University of Texas at Austin, Geoffrey is known best locally as the author of feature articles and the monthly "Top Drawer" column in the magazine *Texas Business,* where he was an associate editor until 1981. In addition, from his base in an 1899 Galveston home, he helps cover the space shuttle program for *Time.* He is a past president of Galveston's Silk Stocking Historic District.

STEPHEN BARNHILL
Editor

Stephen Barnhill, a third-generation Houstonian, attended undergraduate schools at the University of Denver and Arizona State University, and went on to do graduate study at Rice University before beginning a six-year tenure as publications editor at Rice in 1973. He left behind those academic surroundings to begin a writing career in advertising and public relations in 1979. Today, he is the principal in Steve Barnhill & Company, a marketing communications firm, and a partner in Taylor Brown & Barnhill Inc., a full-service, Houston-based advertising agency.

JERRY HERRING
Designer

Jerry Herring, born in Iowa, attended the Minneapolis School of Art and the Kansas City Art Institute. *Print* Magazine named Jerry one of the nation's 12 most promising young designers before he graduated in 1969. Thereafter, until 1971, Jerry worked for Stan Richards & Associates, a Dallas graphic design firm. He moved to Houston in 1971 and worked with Baxter & Korge and the Kelvin Group Partnership before forming his own firm, Herring Design, in 1973. His studio now ranks among Texas's most respected and most decorated in national and international design competitions.

DANCIE PERUGINI WARE
Producer

A fifth-generation Galvestonian, Dancie Perugini Ware has been intimately associated with the preservation movement in Galveston since 1973. She is a graduate of the University of Texas at Austin and did post-graduate work at the University of Perugina, Italy. Since graduation, Dancie has been successfully publicizing the renaissance of Galveston through features in local and national media. She presently directs public relations and special projects for George Mitchell Interests and is an independent public relations consultant.

Kauffman & Runge
1881–82

Sweeney-Royston House
1885

Heidenheimer-Marine
Building
1875

FOREWORD

Previous publications have, with great architectural respect, revealed Galveston's past. This book is a documentation of the emerging Galveston of the future.

The towns and islands of the Texas Gulf Coast boast many miles of sandy beaches, where dreamers enjoy balmy breezes as they watch a moonrise over the waters, and sunworshippers and youthful builders of sand castles revel under bright summer skies. The swimmers, snorkelers, skin divers, surfers, and sailors experience the separateness that only an ocean can provide. The fishermen angle for excitement or for a meal or for a living, and picnicking families fire charcoal for hamburgers or hot dogs or fresh-caught crabs.

These images Galveston shares with dozens of communities between Mexico and Louisiana. But Galveston alone bespeaks a history of such fame and fortune that, before the devastating 1900 hurricane, she was known as the "Wall Street of the Southwest." Galveston alone among Texas coastal towns can boast an unparalleled collection of Victorian homes and iron-front buildings from the middle-to-late 19th century.

During the last several decades, however, demolition crews, assisted with regularity by destructive hurricanes, have gradually but decisively razed a building here, a home there. The cry for preservation came too late for some architectural treasures, but many, as you will see here, have survived. A new Galveston conscience is at work, lovingly restoring the once-dying beauty. The Galveston of past glory is experiencing a renaissance.

In the manner of archeologists who chip painstakingly at layer after layer of surface soil to unearth priceless antiquities, today's planners, architects and restoration specialists, engineers and builders, artisans and craftsmen are working together to strip from aging Galveston structures the veil of dust and decay and, all too frequently, the ill-conceived "remodelling" efforts of bygone days to recreate the lively facades. The Galveston that was is becoming the Galveston that is. The history we extol is the hallmark of Galveston's future.

Join us in our celebration.

Cynthia Mitchell
1985

Hutchings Sealy Bank Building
1895

Ashton Villa
1858

Walter Gresham House
(The Bishop's Palace)
1887–93

INTRODUCTION

Architecture, like government, is about as good as a community deserves. The shell which we create for ourselves marks our spiritual development as plainly as that of a snail denotes its species.

Lewis Mumford

Throughout its history, Galveston Island has been on the fringe. The two miles that divide it from the Texas mainland cannot describe the psychic cleft between Galveston and the state and nation that claimed it. French pirate Jean Laffite found the island to be a convenient refuge just beyond U.S. jurisdiction in the early 19th century. Later, the Confederacy deemed it indefensible because of its vulnerability to the guns of the blockading Federal fleet, and it ultimately became the only major city in Texas to fall into Union hands. In the 20th century, when the island was a safe harbor for gambling, prostitution, and other vices, mainland Texans dismissed such illicit activities by explaining that Galveston was not really a part of Texas.

Island cities *are* different. There is the omnipresence of water. There is a feeling of isolation. Furthermore, a curious history has left Galveston, a barrier island merely 50 miles south of Houston, a time capsule of the 19th century. Transient prosperity, the subtropical climate, a large immigrant population, and the currents of Victorian fashion gave the island its own special architectural character. And geography to the contrary, Galveston has long been the most Southern of all Texas cities.

Galveston doesn't even appear to belong in Texas. Rather, it looks as if it had been swept away from the Deep South in some grandiose storm and deposited on the Texas Gulf Coast. The tropical flora—palm trees, oleanders, magnolias—belie the image of the Great Plains. The island's moisture-laden heat is as palpable as white cream gravy. Moreover, few cities in Texas or the Southwest have blacks and whites living so close together. Hundreds of residential blocks on Galveston's east end have for many decades been racially integrated, if economically divided. And pedestrians, a Texas rarity, can be seen almost everywhere. Because of its size, Galveston is a place where walking remains a practical means of getting around.

Even the earliest visitors could sense a difference here. "Galveston is [in] a position of much more importance than the Government hitherto supposed—It is the key to the greatest

and best part of the province of Texas," wrote a U.S. presidential envoy who visited the island in 1818.[1] Unlock the vast, rich territory, evict the smugglers, and encourage American settlement, he urged.

The U.S. Government ignored its envoy's recommendations. But his promise of greatness for the island would nonetheless be fulfilled. Galveston became the "Queen City" of Texas by mid-century and remained so for 50 years. During that span, it was the center of trade, finance, and culture in Texas. Its prosperous citizenry was eager to show off its wealth and express its notions of elegance by building impressive homes and commercial houses. And build it did, putting talents and tastes from around the world to work shaping grand structures. Yet nature, too, became the island's architect. In the year 1900, Galveston's great natural resource, the Gulf of Mexico, rose up, shattered the city, and killed 6,000 of its inhabitants. But the toll was greater still, for the storm of 1900 washed away not only life and prosperity, but also Galveston's visions of grandeur.

After the hurricane and accompanying tidal wave, the city was overwhelmed by the tasks of rebuilding, erecting a seawall, and raising the ground level of the entire east end of the island. Little time or money was available to allow Galveston to keep pace with its rival to the north, Houston, which had its own grand plans. As a result, the island's economy slipped into the doldrums, where it stayed for much of the 20th century. The city's population in 1980 was 62,000, virtually unchanged since 1940, and only 24,000 more than the 1900 census.

However, all was not lost. Along with the charms of barrier island living, much of the rich 19th century architecture survived. Neither furies of nature nor economics could destroy it. Indeed, Galveston's floundering economy kept the wrecking balls at bay, and so is in large part responsible for the treasure trove of Victorian architecture that escaped urban renewal. In more recent years, preservationists have played a complementary role by demonstrating the value of Galveston's historic architecture to tourism. Since 1970, scores of structures have been painstakingly restored or given new life through adaptive rehabilitation. Many of the island's fine examples of Greek Revival, Romanesque, Gothic, Italianate, and Queen Anne architecture now stand reinstated to their former splendor and ready to face the next century.

George Sealy House
1887–89

Ashbel Smith Building
(Old Red)
1890

Sacred Heart Church
1903–4

Galveston owes its existence to a quirk of nature. Shallow water thwarts seafaring traffic along most of the 624-mile Texas coast. But between the eastern tip of Galveston Island and the Bolivar Peninsula, strong currents were found to keep the pass from shoaling. That slip of water became the link between Galveston, a narrow 32-mile-long island, and the rest of the 19th century world.

European explorers had stumbled upon the island numerous times. Galveston is believed to be the island where Cabeza de Vaca was shipwrecked in 1528. Its name comes from the Spanish governor of Louisiana, Bernardo de Galvez, who commissioned a survey of the Texas Coast in 1783. The surveyors named the largest bay they encountered in honor of the governor, and the barrier island became known as *Galvezton*.

Jean Laffite, Galveston's first distinguished entrepreneur, understood the island's virtues. After being driven from his outpost near New Orleans by the U.S. Navy, the French pirate established a village on Galveston in 1817. Here, Laffite, who maintained he was not a pirate but an ambitious privateer, was able to prey on foreign vessels in the Gulf and then retreat beyond the reach of U.S. law. After members of his colony attacked American ships, however, U.S. naval forces intervened and evicted Laffite from the island. The celebrated buccaneer left his sanctuary in 1821, the same year that Mexico won independence from Spain.

The fledgling Government of Mexico largely ignored its island territory of Galveston. Texas entrepreneur Michel B. Menard showed more interest. He devised a scheme to gain title to the eastern part of the island as a business venture. Secretly using a native Mexican as his representative, Menard purchased a *league* (4,428 acres) and a *labor* (177 acres) on the island in 1834. The next year, merchant Thomas F. McKinney became Menard's partner in the endeavor. Their larger plans were complicated by the Texas revolution against Mexico in 1836. Later that year, the new congress of the Republic of Texas required the two entrepreneurs to bid anew for the Galveston land, and they were successful with an offer of $50,000.

The Galveston City Company, launched by Menard and McKinney, quickly began selling lots and promoting the harbor. An "astonishing" building boom commenced. "The rapidity with which these houses are run up is inconceivable," wrote one visitor. Another observed that Galveston seemed "destined to be the New York of Texas."[2]

Galveston's harbor became the focal point for almost all trade going in and out of rapidly developing Texas. Dry goods, manufactured items, building materials, railroad iron, and virtually everything else necessary to life in the state came over the island's wharves. The returning ships, bound

Merchants Mutual Insurance
Company Building
1870

for New Orleans, the Eastern Seaboard, and Europe, were frequently loaded with cotton, far and away the state's most important export.

The city also became a center for finance. Because banking was outlawed in Texas from the inception of the Republic until after the Civil War, cotton factoring and commission houses performed most banking services, though their activity was certainly of questionable legality. The Commercial and Agricultural Bank, whose owners argued that their pre-revolution Mexican charter took precedence over the Texas ban, and the trading firm of R. & D. G. Mills kept their own commercial paper in circulation all over the coast, where it was honored in lieu of gold.

Islanders also did a brisk business in the outfitting of ships and in the selling of marine and fire insurance. Some manufacturing also was established. There were iron foundries, a rope factory, a soap factory, a book bindery, printing companies, and several newspapers, the largest of which, the *Galveston News* (later, the *Galveston Daily News*), had statewide influence because of its large circulation on the mainland.

The population grew from just under 14,000 in 1870 to 22,000 in 1880, and by 1890 the city reached 29,000. Post-war Galveston was booming. In 1873, the island had at least nine newspapers. The *Daily News,* the *Civilian,* the *Mercury,* and the *Times* published general news. The *Spectator* had a Republican orientation, while the *Texas Post* and the *Unabhangige* were published in German. The *Texas New Yorker* covered business news, and the *Texas Christian Advocate* treated religious affairs.[3]

By 1887, the city's seven banks were conducting more than $71 million in transactions for the year. Galveston had 10 insurance companies and was served by four railroads. The port received 183 foreign vessels and 426 transient vessels in 1885. That same year, the city's 47 wholesalers traded $12.5 million in groceries, $1.1 million in shoes and hats, $1.1 million in liquor, and $1.5 million in coffee. Galveston was indeed the grand emporium of Texas.

A grip on Texas trade—inbound raw materials, commodities, and manufactured goods; outbound cotton and grain—fostered great wealth in Galveston. Its well-travelled citizenry put much stock in creating the appearance of refinement. The wealthy were compulsive about building splendid houses, grandiose buildings, and temples devoted to the arts. Philadelphian Samuel Sloan, a prominent 19th-century architect, wrote: "Southerners have been known to travel fifteen hundred miles to see a handsome new house. The next thing was to outdo it, at whatever expense, and in this they generally succeeded."[4]

Sloan's comment was certainly true of privileged Galvestonians, whose maritime interests permitted them to comb the world for rich materials and furnishings for their island palaces. Shipper H. A. Landes, for instance, was so impressed

Frederick Beissner House
1887

by Spanish hand-tooled leather that he is said to have shipped fine leathers as well as artisans from Spain to embellish the wainscoting of his large Romanesque home, built in 1887. Thirty years earlier, Captain J. M. Brown had brought in brick from Philadelphia, hand-carved walnut window valances from Paris, and French artisans to adorn his Ashton Villa interior with friezes, moldings, and ceiling medallions of gold leaf. When George Sealy built his home, The Open Gates, in 1888-89, he arranged for the brick and terra-cotta ornaments to come from Belgium, the mahogany paneling from Honduras, and the silver light fixtures from England.

Extravagances poured into the city. In 1858 alone, Galvestonians purchased 23 grand pianos, $2,490 worth of silver plate, 3,665 gallons of French wine, and 786 gallons of French brandy. During the prior year, the British Consul at Galveston complained that the opulent lifestyle maintained by the average family of the mercantile class on the island was so high that he found it impossible to maintain any semblance of social reciprocity. He reported to London that the standard of living "was dearer at this port" than at any other in the United States.[5]

In the pre-Civil War years, when much of the domestic help was provided by slaves, even the servants did not escape the indulgent life. British Lieutenant Colonel James Fremantle, visiting the island during the war in the early 1860s, observed with amazement in the pages of his diary: "innumerable Negroes and Negresses parading about the streets in the most outrageously grand costumes—silks, satins, crinolines, hats with feathers, lace mantles, etc., forming an absurd contrast to the simple dresses of their mistresses. Many were driving about in their masters' carriages." Evidently, the contrast between slave and mistress was enhanced by the restraint shown by the wealthy when in public. Fancy dress was appropriate in private, yet considered bad form for the street. Festooning one's servants, it appears, was an acceptable substitute.

Perhaps even more than other luxuries, architecture enthralled Galvestonians. As a trading rival, Houston was a formidable opponent. But when it came to architectural ostentation, the "Bayou City" was no match for Galveston.

ELLIS ISLAND OF THE WEST

"The population boasts members of every nation. English, American, German, Italian, Dutch, etc.," remarked a foreign visitor to Galveston in 1840. A French traveler in 1857 was equally impressed, writing that the city possessed the most "heterogeneous" citizenry he had encountered anywhere, noting that on the streets of Galveston he met immigrants from Germany, Spain, France, Italy, and Ireland.[6]

As a port of entry, the island received thousands of immigrants. Though most moved inland, many stayed on at

Galveston, where tradesmen found that business opportunities were abundant.

The ethnic stew that Galveston became had a profound effect on its architecture. While the aristocracy was heavily influenced by the oscillating standards of Victorian taste, the *nouveau riche* immigrants imported their own concepts of opulence. Hence, Wurtenberg-native Samson Heidenheimer could build his 37-room Heidenheimer Castle with as much emphasis on the statement it would make in the Old World as in his adopted land. In the same way, John Clement Trube, who left a job as gardener for a nobleman in Denmark, built a house based on a Danish castle without fretting about its compliance with current fashion. These men had achieved success, and their homes were celebrations of their good fortune.

Notwithstanding the prominence of the immigrants, wealthy Americans were at the top of the social hierarchy of 19th-century Galveston. Men such as Robert Mills, who was born to a rich Kentucky planter and educated at the University of Tennessee, and Col. W.L. Moody, a Virginia-born lawyer and cotton merchant, exemplified the local gentry.

Another social orbit, separate yet well-regarded, was populated by the many prosperous Germans. Their community supported its own churches, newspapers, social clubs, and even the German Reading Room, which was tended by a full-time librarian. Two German cultural groups erected their own buildings in 1859 to accommodate social gatherings and theatrical productions. The enormous Garten Verein Pavilion was built in 1876 for still another German social club. It became fashionable for non-German families to enjoy dancing, bowling, tennis, and croquet at the Garten Verein as guests of the club's members.

While the prospect of religious and political freedom attracted many Germans, Texas's cheap land and fertile business opportunities were even greater incentives. European shipping firms fueled emigration by printing guidebooks for distribution in Germany that recommended Galveston as a place to begin anew. According to the *Galveston Daily News,* two of the island's transplanted Germans went so far as to order a 700-ton ship built in Bremen "especially for the emigration trade to Galveston" in 1856.

Reports of Galveston's promising future also drew Eastern European Jews, who were being persecuted in Prague and Budapest. For Jews, in fact, the island city's reputation as a desirable immigration point survived the 1800s. Thousands fled the pogroms of Russia for the island rather than the Jewish ghettos of New York in the early 20th century, inspiring the title of historian Bernard Marinbach's book, *Galveston: Ellis Island of the West.*[7]

Germans and European Jews were only two ingredients in the island's ethnic stew, as any list of Galveston's leading 19th-century citizens reveals. The founder of the city, Michel

Menard, was a Canadian who did not learn English until he was a young man. The prosperous Galveston bakery owner Andrew Baldinger was Swiss. Judge J. L. Darragh, president of the powerful Wharf Company, was from Ireland. Morritz Kopperl, president of the National Bank of Texas and the Gulf, Colorado & Santa Fe Railroad, was from Moravia. Prominent merchants Leon Blum, J. M. Walthew, and Victor Baulard came, respectively, from Alsace, England, and France. The work of Alfred Muller, an architect and German immigrant who designed Old City Hall, the Trube House, and other buildings, bears a strong imprint of his European background. And the list goes on.

Immigrants were particularly important to the building trades. Galveston was without resident architects until the 1870s. Thus, many of the aesthetic details of construction were left to the European carpenters and masons who were performing the work. In many cases, these craftsmen, who brought an eye for grace and proportion from the Old World, were responsible for the beauty of early Galveston buildings, as well as the vernacular architecture of the entire century. And after the arrival of architects with commissions to create the island's grandest buildings, it was often the immigrant stonecutters and masons, particularly the Germans, who executed the intricate designs.

THE THREAT FROM THE SEA

From the beginning, nature, too, exerted a profound influence on Galveston's architecture. The highest part of the island in 1840 was only five feet above sea level, a fact that caused a variety of hardships. Francis Sheridan wrote in 1940: "The nature of the soil on which Galveston is built...a mixture of mud & sand generally up to the ankles of the pedestrian...is productive of various complaints, such as Yellow Fever, Ague, Rheumatisms &c, for when either from a heavy fall of rain, or an irruption of the sea, the ground gets thoroughly soaked, the effect of the hot sun extracts such a horrible stench as no ordinary nose has smelt—In addition, there is nothing fragrant in dead and decaying oysters which plentifully bestrew the streets."[8]

Islanders combatted the high tides of the Gulf by building their structures on brick piers, usually three to ten feet above ground. This technique also improved air circulation within the homes and buildings, a paramount concern in the subtropical heat. The typical Galveston home of the period had one and a half or two stories, with high ceilings, dozens of windows, and often two or three verandas from which to take advantage of the Gulf breezes. The most common design featured double galleries, or porches, on the front of the house and usually at least a small gallery at the rear. North-facing houses often also had huge rear galleries from which to take advantage of the frequent breezes from the south. Almost all

THE FIRST NATIONAL BANK
OF GALVESTON

windows had double-hung sashes, so that they could be opened at both the top and bottom for better ventilation. Window openings onto galleries frequently spanned from floor to ceiling, thus serving as both window and door. Wood shutters were made for nearly every window and could be used for screening the afternoon sun as well as for storm protection. Tall towers, or cupolas, were sometimes used to draw warm air out of a house.

The double gallery was not only practical, but it also could be melded with Greek Revival style, which in one form or another flourished in Galveston throughout the last half of the 19th century. So well suited to the local climate were elements of Greek Revival that they invaded the Italianate, Second Empire, and Romanesque styles that came later in the century.

The need to raise houses off the ground gave Galveston a vertical orientation, which was accentuated because land on the small island was precious. People built up instead of out. Many of the surviving structures are so tall and the streets so narrow that one must retreat several hundred feet to observe an entire front elevation.

The weather that so influenced the buildings of Galveston periodically cast uncertainty on the city's ability to survive. Storms in 1837, 1841, and 1842 set back the infant city. In 1839 and 1844, yellow fever killed hundreds of townspeople. But in spite of it all, the building and population boom continued. The Civil War and several catastrophic fires crippled the city later, yet Galveston's phenomenal vitality endured. Unlike many Southern cities, Texas's island city enjoyed immense prosperity after Appomattox.

Josiah Gregg, an early traveler, cautioned that the island could be in jeopardy if a prolonged wind blew from the "south or southeast and a full tide happened at the conclusion." The sea might "rise over the coast," he warned. Such predictions were repeated from time to time, but the island, defenseless against war and the sea, prevailed.

THE APPALLING CALAMITY OF MODERN TIMES

On the morning of September 8, 1900, Isaac Cline, chief of the local weather bureau, grew alarmed by the falling barometer. Mounting his horse-drawn cart, Cline hurriedly rode through the city, urging people to leave the island. By midday, the bridges to the mainland were under water, and the 38,000 residents of Galveston were trapped.

As the day wore on, water filled the streets. Houses near the beach were swept away, and the weather bureau's wind gauge blew away. Houses soon began lurching from their foundations, while others simply blew apart. A maelstrom of debris immediately moved north, wrecking those homes and buildings in its path. Roofing slates became deadly missiles. People were swept out of second-story windows.

By morning, 6,000 people were dead, 3,600 homes were destroyed, and 10,000 survivors were homeless. The 1900 storm was, and remains today, the most deadly natural disaster in U.S. history.

In the wake of the storm, some 6,000 surviving residents gave up on Galveston and left the island forever. It is a testimonial to the fortitude and optimism of those townspeople who stayed that Galveston was rebuilt. The hurricane left the island with no utilities, no bridges to the mainland, and tons upon tons of wreckage. The task of disposing of the bodies was so great that heaps of corpses were loaded on barges for burial at sea, while others were piled high in the streets and burned. Reported one witness: "Galveston is almost wiped off the earth."

Determined to make Galveston less vulnerable, the residents not only rebuilt, but also performed two amazing feats. Beginning in 1902, they used a new railroad from the mainland to haul in 13,000 rail carloads of rock and other materials for the construction of a seawall. The first section of the wall, which rose 17 feet above ground, required 5,200 rail cars of crushed granite, 1,800 cars of sand, 1,000 cars of cement, 1,600 cars of 45-foot wood pilings, 3,700 cars of granite chunks from a quarry 220 miles inland, and 5 cars of steel rods. This seawall extended down the beach for three and a half miles.

The seawall was extended in 1918 and several times hence. It is now 10.4 miles in length.

In 1904, a second monumental task was begun. The entire city was elevated. This effort, commonly referred to as the grade raising of Galveston, elevated the city an average of 10 feet. Canals were dug through city streets and ocean-going dredges were floated into them to spew fill material everywhere. Hundreds of buildings on the island had to be jacked up 10 feet or more during the grade raising. Photographs of the era show enormous buildings, including St. Patrick's Church and the mansion at Avenue O and 28th Street, in what appears to be a state of levitation, when actually the buildings were floating on scores of screw jacks, which were turned by scores of men. A drum was used to synchronize the effort, each man turning his jack a quarter turn per drumbeat. During the six-year project, residents navigated the streets via wooden catwalks built above the canals and the 14 million cubic yards of wet sand that was pumped in from the Gulf. The grade raising killed all the trees and plantings that survived the storm. The thousands of trees and lush vegetation one sees today were planted after 1905.

The rebuilding of Galveston was not something taken for granted at the time. Many people, and certainly most of the 6,000 residents who moved away after the 1900 storm, sincerely believed that Galveston had no future. But for the spirit and tenacity of its remaining citizenry, Galveston would have died a lingering death after the great storm. The

busy port of Indianola on Matagorda Bay, a hundred miles west of Galveston, was destroyed by a hurricane in 1886. Indianola was not rebuilt, and today there is scarcely any evidence of its former existence.

THE GALVESTON STYLE

In the early 1800s, the U.S. subtly began transforming itself from an agricultural society to the industrial power it would become by the end of the century. In architecture, America the hayseed longed for Old World sophistication. The Greek style, with its grand proportions and Classic pedigree, was eagerly embraced. A "Greek Revival" swept across America, manifested in the public buildings and fashionable residences of nearly every city and town.

For a new city in the fledgling Republic of Texas, a city being constructed on a heretofore ignored sandspit in the Gulf of Mexico, the Greek style had great appeal. When Augustus Allen, a founder of Houston, built the Menard House in 1838, its display of Classicism launched Galveston on the road to aesthetic refinement. Another Galveston City Company stockholder, Samuel May Williams, built a simpler house bearing many of the trademarks of Greek Revival the following year. The Williams House greatly resembles the plantation houses built in southern Louisiana and New Orleans, where the entrepreneur lived prior to sailing for Texas.

The popularity of the Greek Revival can be in part attributed to the fact that it was easily mimicked in the hinterlands. Architect Drury Blakely Alexander wrote: "It brought a harmony and dignity to the simplest farm house, as well as elegance to the great mansion. The Early Texas house, with its row of posts across the front supporting a roof, was with very little effort transformed into a simple Greek Revival house. The builder had only to enlarge the posts or columns and add a few moldings or strips at the top and then surmount this with a proportionately heavier beam or entablature and top the whole thing with a simple cornice."[10]

The use of columns created the large galleries that would come to characterize what is now called the "Galveston Style." Houses in Galveston were often constructed of wood that had been used as ballast for ships returning to the island after delivering cotton to other ports on the Gulf or the Eastern Seaboard. Cypress, which is particularly resistant to wood rot, was a common building material.

In many areas of the nation, the Greek Revival began to fade around the middle of the century. By the Civil War, it had fallen out of favor in the East. But because it proved so practical for the local climate and so adaptable to succeeding fashions, the Greek Revival had a particularly long tenure on the island. Simple vernacular houses, with double galleries, low-hipped roofs, and minor Victorian deviations, were built in large numbers until the turn of the century.

Lemuel Burr House
1876

Few of Galveston's surviving commercial buildings are strict Greek Revival. The Customs House and, to some extent, Hendley Row, are examples. But by the time the use of brick and iron afforded a degree of permanence to commercial buildings, the varied themes of the later Victorian period had superseded the Greek. Because most of the iron fronts used in Galveston were ordered from foundries in the East, where architectural fashion arrived much earlier than on the island, the houses of commerce were more contemporary in style than residential structures. The standard commercial building fronts ordered from catalogs arrived cast in iron and subject to little or no provincial influence.

"The early Victorians were convinced that 'architecture is an art in which Italy has no modern rival'...No wonder, gentlemen of means who aspired to culture were eager to enjoy some of this Italian refinement in their own homes," wrote John Maass in *The Gingerbread Age*.[11] Merchant James M. Brown, a gentleman of considerable means, erected Galveston's first Italian villa in 1858. Ashton Villa was a bold departure from Greek Revival, and surely this grand home paved the way for the more modest, wooden Italianate residences that followed. The Garnett House and the Everett House, pictured later in this volume, are two of only a handful that have survived.

As Ashton Villa was being completed, tremors of secession were already moving through the South. The Civil War and the Union blockade brought construction, so dependent on the shipping trade, to a halt. However, Galveston quickly recovered. After the war, Victorian architecture flowered on the island.

THE GILDED ERA

Queen Victoria took the throne at the age of 18 in 1837. Coincident to this, a procession of revivals began that influenced art, literature, and architecture. The industrial age was underway. Living standards rose, and fashion once again looked to the past for guidance in matters of style. The complex and unpredictable Victorian styles liberated 19th century builders from the confines of the Greek rectangle.

The Austin-Fox House in Galveston is a beautiful example of the transition style. The double gallery of eclectic columns and the general design suggest Greek Revival, while the large, elaborate double corbels borrow from the Italianate, and the richly carved gingerbread brackets reflect the Gothic Revival. "When Gothic was translated into 'Carpenter Gothic,' the stone tracery became wooden 'gingerbread,'" writes Maass.[12] Like the Greek double gallery, gingerbread was well received, and it became an important element of the Galveston Style. Because carpenters and wood were more plentiful than stonecutters and limestone, gingerbread was a practical embellishment for simple structures. The ginger-

bread trim on these homes today forms a catalog of literally hundreds of different examples of Victorian shapes. The same fanciful patterns permeated the Victorian world and were translated into furniture, needlework, newspaper advertisements, fences, signs, steamboats, and for the less fortunate Victorians, tombs.

During the decade following 1885, the full range of Victorian style was represented in Galveston. The wildly exuberant Carpenter Gothic Sonnentheil House, the fortress-like Romanesque Landes House, the monumental Renaissance Revival Bishop's Palace, the bizarre Trube House, and the Wolfe House, a softly asymmetrical Queen Anne home based on a floral motif, were all constructed during this 10-year span. It was an energetic time, and styles fell in and out of favor at a dizzying pace. Eclecticism, a philosophy whose adherents sought to adopt the most appealing aspects of various disparate styles and theories, thrived.

Meanwhile, architects had set up practices on the island, and commercial buildings and the larger homes were created with the added finesse of trained designers. Nicholas Clayton, an Irish-born architect educated in America, became the architect of choice and won the commissions for numerous offices, institutional buildings, and residences. Clayton designed the Greenleve, Block & Co., the Trueheart-Adriance, the W. L. Moody, and the Hutchings Sealy Bank buildings. His designs exhibit a strong sense of style and imagination. Because of his uniformly high standard of work and prolific output, Clayton contributed more to architecture in Galveston than anyone else during the last quarter of the 19th century.

As the century came to a close, the Renaissance became the model for the grand houses of the rich. In one of the last architectural splurges before the 1900 storm, George Sealy had the prestigious New York firm of McKim, Meade & White design a huge mansion, an Italian Renaissance extravaganza he named "The Open Gates."

In addition to including homes and buildings constructed prior to 1900, this volume includes six buildings from the 20th century. Some are based on revivals of past themes, while others, such as the Lucas Terraces apartment house of 1902-8, usher in new concepts altogether. The Lucas Terraces is a wonderful expression of *art nouveau.* Its curious window boxes, which are shaped like seashells with coral-like railings, suggest the organic patterns of Antoni Gaudi's Casa Mila Apartment House in Barcelona. Across the street from the Lucas Terraces stands Sacred Heart Church, a Moorish-inspired replacement for the large Romanesque church destroyed by the 1900 storm. Sacred Heart was built in 1903–4.

The Spanish Revival is represented on these pages by the Galvez Hotel, completed in 1911, and the Daniel Kempner House, built in 1907. The Classical Revival, which had such

a profound influence on Victorian Galveston, was reawakened in the closing years of the 19th century and remained popular well into the next. The City National Bank Building of 1919–20 exemplifies the Neo-Classical movement.

Finally, anchoring the west end of The Strand, as if to waken the pedestrian from his 19th-century trance, is the brilliant white art deco Santa Fe Building, built in 1931–32. Though the clean lines of this Jazz Age ziggurat reject the sumptuous curves of the 19th century, the Santa Fe Building gracefully coexists with its neighbors.

DECLINE AND RENEWAL

The rebuilding that followed the 1900 storm consumed much of the energy and resources of the people of Galveston for years. Meanwhile, the railroad hub of Houston was further developing its own ship channel and port. The Queen City languished as a commercial center and grew more dependent on, and more corrupted by, the resort industry of that time. During Prohibition, Galveston flourished as an entertainment mecca. Gambling, prostitution, and, of course, booze, were readily available to those wishing to escape the fundamentalism of the Texas Bible Belt for a few days. After Repeal, casino gambling replaced bootlegging as a major local industry. Gaming houses, such as the Turf Club, the Balinese Room, and the Hollywood Club, attracted thousands of tourists to see the entertainers of the day. Guy Lombardo, Phil Harris, and Duke Ellington were among the many luminaries who performed on the island.

In 1957, the Texas attorney general shut down the gambling houses, and Galveston was dealt another blow. From the 1950s to the 1980s, the population and the economy remained stagnant. Yet these years served an important purpose. They cleansed the soul of Galveston of its grand pretensions, so that the island was no longer haunted by its halcyon days. Most people on the island today never saw the Queen City of the Gulf. They do not measure the city by the standards of the last century. They are not stalked by the memory of streets lined with opulent palaces and grand public halls. The island citizenry today can accept that Galveston has a different role to play.

Paradoxically, it was the emergence of a historical and preservation movement that released Galveston from its past. The island's history is now a source of community pride. Rather than serving as a grim reminder of the city's decline, it offers the promise of better years to come.

Thirty years of neglect yielded valuable dividends: Hundreds of Victorian homes and buildings were left untouched. As John Gunther put it, the city remained "something like a fly in amber—not decayed, but arrested." In cities with healthier economies throughout the country, much of the fine architecture of the last century was razed to accommodate growth.

John Darragh House
1888–89

While Galvestonians in general were slow to appreciate this resource until the 1970s, a few preservation-minded individuals made important stands earlier. In 1954, members of what was then called the Galveston Historical Society acquired the 1839 Samuel May Williams House and saved it from destruction. The group then reorganized and incorporated as the Galveston Historical Foundation. In 1969, when Ashton Villa appeared to be headed for demolition, the group intervened and ultimately purchased the mansion. About the same time, the Junior League of Galveston bought and restored the 1881 Trueheart-Adriance Building near The Strand. Washington-based preservation lawyer Peter Brink was hired as its executive in 1973. In the ensuing years, Brink was instrumental in creating the Strand Revolving Fund, the initial contributions to which came from the Moody Foundation and the Kempner Fund. The Revolving Fund was used to acquire historic buildings on The Strand, which were then protected by deed restrictions ensuring the preservation of each building's character. Thereafter, the buildings were sold to private developers.

The East End Historical District was established in 1971. However, efforts to create a similar district that year in The Strand area failed in city council. The Silk Stocking Historic District was established by the city in 1975. An annual homes tour, sponsored by the Historical Foundation, increased interest in residential preservation, and the restoration of scores of Victorian homes was begun.

With the success of a few key merchants located on The Strand, preservation efforts there gained momentum, and the forces of the marketplace slowly took over. By the 1980's The Strand had become a major tourist attraction, and private developers no longer had to be convinced that businesses could survive in an area that had been relegated to a warehouse district only a few years before.

Today, most of the buildings on The Strand are occupied and well maintained, and preservation activity has spread to the surrounding streets. Hundreds of 19th-century homes have been beautifully restored in several thriving residential neighborhoods in the east end. By perserving its heritage, Galveston has come to be perceived—both on and off the island—as a small but vibrant city with special charms. And Galveston shares those charms with an increasing number of visitors each year. Historic Galveston, the city's legacy of its colorful past, is now a major attraction, and an important part of Galveston's future.

Leon & H. Blum Building
(The Tremont House)
1879–80, 1882

Old Galveston Customs House
1858–61

Landes House
1887

Thomas Jefferson
League Building
1871–72

Mallory Building
1878

Lucas Terraces
1902–8

McDonald House
1889 or 1890

Garten Verein Dancing
Pavilion
1876 ◆ ◆ ◆

First Presbyterian Church
1872–89

Santa Fe Railroad Building
(Shearn Moody Plaza)
1931–32

Joel B. Wolfe House
Circa 1894

1
MICHEL MENARD HOUSE
1838–39
1605 33rd Street

Mary Jane Menard, third wife of Michel Menard, described the couple's home in a letter to a friend dated October 30, 1844: "We live about half a mile from town, half a mile from the Gulf, a mile from the bay, and three miles from the East end of the Island or pass. Our home is large with upper and lower galleries, a store room…kitchen, servent [*sic*] rooms, stable, and carriage house and last not least a chicken house in which I raised with my own hands (not the negroes), 73 chickens and had as many eggs as my family could use."[13]

Michel Brindamour Menard founded the city of Galveston. Born near Montreal in 1805, he spent his years before coming to Texas engaged in a number of trades, including fur packing in Canada, lumber rafting along the Illinois and Mississippi rivers, and Indian trading in Arkansas. After moving his trading business to Nacogdoches, Texas, Menard became involved in politics. He signed the Texas Declaration of Independence in 1836 and represented the new Republic in negotiations with the Indians. Later that year, he purchased the east end of Galveston Island from the first congress of the Republic. He soon organized the Galveston City Company and began selling stock and property.

For many years it was believed that Menard had built this Greek Revival house on 33rd Street. However, research during the 1966 Historic American Buildings Survey revealed that the house was erected by Augustus Chapman Allen, who founded Houston with his brother John Kirby Allen. Menard and his wife Mary Jane apparently moved to the house in 1843.

Menard and the latter two of his four wives held many lavish parties at the house. A masquerade ball first held here in 1853 evolved into the annual Mardi Gras festivities that are observed in Galveston to this day. Menard died in 1856. Around 1879 the house was purchased by Captain Edward Ketchum, whose family occupied it until 1977.[14]

The house has a straightforward Greek Revival design. The building materials were shipped as ballast from Maine. The original house is thought to have been partially prefabricated, with the beams and other elements marked for simple assembly. According to a member of the Ketchum family, the column bases of the main gallery rotted away, requiring the addition of the present box bases. The wings to the north and south are not original. Because of the many trees on the spacious grounds, Menard called his home "The Oaks." With its tall Ionic columns and graceful lines, The Oaks is a good example of the dignity that the Greek style brought to essentially simple homes of the early Texas Republic.

2
SAMUEL MAY WILLIAMS HOUSE
1839
3601 Avenue P

The Williams House is a typical Greek Revival adaptation of the Louisiana plantation-style residence. Storms and fires have destroyed most of the early Galveston structures, but this house is one of the few survivors of what was then a frontier town. The Classical Revival design includes a front gallery supported by Tuscan wood columns, a hip roof with a cupola and rooftop walkway, and plain wood railings on the porch and roof deck. Single dormers face the front and rear, while two dormers face north and two south. To thwart the town's frequent flooding, the house was originally elevated 10 feet above the ground on brick piers.

While the house holds interest as a fine example of an early Galveston residence, the colorful life of its original owner lends it even greater historical significance. Samuel May Williams came to Texas under an assumed name. Historian Margaret Swett Henson explains: "The Panic of 1819 forced many debtors to abandon their farms and homes and to seek a new beginning beyond the reach of the law. By 1822, many of these unfortunate people learned that Mexican Texas offered an asylum from the enforcement of the harsh debtor laws. Chalking "G.T.T." (Gone to Texas) on the door or the gate, the defaulter and his family would steal away." Indeed, in 1822, Williams, who was born in Rhode Island in 1795, quietly boarded a sloop in New Orleans bound for Texas, where he would remain a fugitive from his lenders for many years.

History, however, would not grant him anonymity. Williams soon teamed up with a neighbor from New Orleans, land promoter Stephen F. Austin. Austin had assumed a land grant made to his father by the Spanish government in 1821. In order to stir up interest in his land, Austin placed advertisements in newspapers of the Mississippi Valley offering men with families 640 acres for 12.5 cents per acre. Because he needed a bilingual clerk to prepare the deeds and other papers for the Mexican government, Austin hired Williams. A command of Spanish and French, experience in the mercantile trade, skills as a clerk, and business acumen combined to make Williams invaluable to Austin.

Williams's cosmopolitan nature and general aloofness made him less popular than Austin. Moreover, resentment of Williams grew because of his practice of accepting a lien on one-half a colonist's land in lieu of one-half the bureaucratic fees necessary to gain title to the land. If the colonist was unable to pay the balance within a year, Williams took the land.

As relations between Mexico and Texas worsened in 1831, Williams was caught between his desire to enjoy the favor of the Mexican government and the grievances he shared with his fellow Texans. As a result, he urged moderation in dealings with Mexico, and this action caused him to be hung in effigy in Brazoria, Texas. After this unpleasantness, Williams began to concentrate on commerce.

Shortly before the war between Mexico and Texas, Williams received a bank charter from Mexican officials, and in 1835 he traveled to New York to sell stock in the venture. While there, he received requests for aid from the provisional Texas government. Williams used his own funds and credit, and those of his brothers and business associates, to send the Texans ships, arms, and ammunition worth some $150,000. The Republic of Texas never fully repaid Williams. Heirs of his business partner, Thomas McKinney, received partial payment from the state in 1935, a hundred years later, but no descendants of Williams came forward to accept his share.

In 1836, McKinney and Menard founded the Galveston City Company. Williams was one of the original directors and investors. Two years later, Williams again left Texas to arrange for the financing and building of six ships that the Texas navy needed to protect the state's coast from Mexican attack. In 1839, Williams was elected to the congress of the Republic. The firm of McKinney and Williams had significant investments in Galveston, including a tavern, the Tremont Hotel, a race track, a warehouse, a wharf, and stables. While Williams attended the congress in Austin, his partner supervised the constuction of a house for the Williams family, then living in San Jacinto. By mid-1840, the house was complete.

Williams and McKinney's business empire grew in size and importance. The two men's claim to a valid bank charter was in dispute for years. However, until his death, Williams was able to fend off legal attacks through the courts and the legislature, and his bank was prosperous. Using the argument that his Mexican charter took precedence over later Texas statutes outlawing banks, Williams was able to print private bank notes that, in effect, served as currency. This practice helped Galveston to flourish as a center of trade, because merchants readily honored "Williams paper," which could be exchanged more easily than scarce gold specie.

Williams enjoyed the fruits of his success. The family home, then located on 20 acres out in the country, was the center of a bustling social life. Williams had nine children, and numerous relatives and visitors enjoyed the family's hospitality. The stable behind the house contained horses and carriages, slaves attended the family and lived in the outbuildings, and the house was furnished with all available comforts. Williams owned tens of thousands of acres of land around the state, a sugar plantation, and considerable property on the island. His merchant house was one of the biggest in the state. Some of Williams's property became the Oakland Plantation, a sugar operation owned by his brothers, Nathaniel and Matthew. The property would later become the site of the Imperial Sugar Company, still doing business in Sugarland, Texas.[15]

Williams died in 1858, six months before the Texas supreme court decided that his bank charter was invalid. Nonetheless regarded as the father of Texas banking, Sam Williams ably served the cause of the Texas Revolution and the young Republic. He spent years away from his family and home in public service. He was also an opportunist who earned many enemies while making his fortune. No doubt this antagonism is in part responsible for the fact that Williams's role in the state's infancy is largely excluded from Texas history.

The cupola and the widow's walk, from which Williams could watch incoming ships and events at his nearby racetrack, burned in the 1890s. They were rebuilt when the house was restored by the Galveston Historical Foundation in 1982. The house now serves as a museum.

—3—
ST. MARY'S CATHEDRAL BASILICA
1847–48, 1884
2011 *Church*

In 1838, a dozen Vincentian priests were dispatched to Texas to serve the faithful. Among the group was The Reverend John Timon. Within four years of arriving, Father Timon raised enough money to build a wood frame church only to see it destroyed by a storm. Clearly a sturdier structure was required, but for it, Galvestonians would have to wait six years.

In 1844, during a yellow fever epidemic, a visiting priest attending the sick was stricken with the disease and died. The next year, as a memorial for use in the construction of a church, the relatives of the priest sent 500,000 bricks from Antwerp, Belgium. When in 1847 Pope Pius IX created the Diocese of Galveston, which included the entire state, he named Father Timon's vice-prefect, John Odin, to be bishop. That same year Bishop Odin

laid the cornerstone for St. Mary's Cathedral. The original structure, including the central nave, side aisles, triforium, transepts, and apse, was completed in 1848.

St. Mary's Cathedral Basilica

Nicholas Clayton, while supervising repairs to the church after a severe storm, added the large tower in 1876. The statue that crowns the tower was erected in 1878. Depicting "Mary, Star of the Sea," the statue that invokes her protection has survived the devastation of the 1900 hurricane and every storm thereafter. Clayton heightened the spires of the front facade to make them proportional to the main tower in 1884.

St. Mary's is the oldest ecclesiastical structure on the island.

John Z. H. Scott House

—4—
JOHN Z. H. SCOTT HOUSE
1850
1721 Broadway

This simple Greek Revival raised cottage was first located at Broadway and 14th Street, where Walter Gresham later built his mansion, now known as the Bishop's Palace. The cottage was moved from the original site to the present location in 1887, when it became the home of John Z. H. Scott. Architect Nicholas Clayton, who designed the Bishop's Palace, also designed a new west wing for Scott.

A Civil War veteran who moved to Galveston from Virginia, Scott worked on the island as a bookkeeper while studying law. Upon completing his study, he entered private practice and later became city attorney. The movie actor Zachary Scott was his grandson.

After Scott's death in 1904, the home remained in the family until 1981, by which time it was in severe disrepair. Mr. and Mrs. Lee Trentham then purchased the house, restored it, and opened a doll museum here in 1982.

—5—
HENDLEY ROW
1855–59
The Strand and 20th Street

On New Year's Day, 1863, Confederate troops drove a Union garrison from Galveston, ending a three-month Federal occupation of the island. During the siege, a Union gunboat shelled The Strand, striking the east side of Hendley Row. The scars of that cannonade are still visible. The capital of the seventh granite column on the 20th Street side remains shattered.

Both Confederate and Federal troops used the rooftop of Hendley Row as an observatory during the war, because it was the highest point in the city.

Hendley Row

Hendley Row was built by William Hendley, a merchant from Connecticut. His firm, William Hendley & Co., founded the Texas and New York Packet Line in order to launch "...a line of fast sailing packets, to ply between this city and New York."[16] Hendley had the materials for his office building shipped from Boston. The *Daily News* recalled the endeavor in a 1908 retrospective: "In command of the vessel *Geranium,* Capt. (John) Quick left Boston during the early part of 1854 for this port, having on board 900 tons of granite, 500 barrels of Rosendale cement, and other building material. The *Geranium,* stated Capt. Quick, drew eleven feet of water when light and was a fine vessel. The bar at the entrance of the harbor at that time...was but 11 feet, so it became necessary to lighter the entire cargo" [i.e., load it onto smaller boats outside the sandbar].[17] Work on the building's foundation was started in 1855, though the row was not completed until 1859.

Within the row are four buildings sharing a common three-story brick facade. The design is largely Greek Revival, with prominent first-story columns, a strong cornice, and symmetrical balance. Granite quoining marks the dividing walls of the four buildings. The nine-foot second-story windows slide up well into the ceiling, permitting access onto a narrow gallery, which originally spanned the entire Strand and 20th Street sides of the row. Granite markers in the center of each building's facade are carved with the date 1858 and the initials of the four original owners, William Hendley, Joseph Hendley, Thomas League, and F. Gilbeau.

William's brother, Joseph Hendley, was a sea captain who commanded the *Star Republic,* the first ship to fly the new flag of the Texas Republic on its voyage from the East Coast to Texas in 1842.[18]

The two buildings of the east end of the row are now occupied by a fruit and produce wholesaler. The next building to the west has been restored and houses a shop on the first floor with apartments above. The west building contains the offices of the Galveston Historical Foundation and The Strand Visitors Center. Hendley Row is the oldest surviving commercial building on The Strand.

6

TRINITY EPISCOPAL CHURCH
1855–57
22nd Street and Winnie

In 1855, the same year that construction began on the Greek Revival Hendley Row buildings, the cornerstone of Trinity Church was laid. To the Victorian mind, the pagan forms that had inspired the Greek Revival were suspect when it came to building Christian churches. Trinity Church represents the Gothic Revival, a style that, rooted in the intensely religious Middle Ages, seemed more spiritual than the Greek.

The facade is dominated by a single tower, which with the floor plan, shows Romanesque influence. But the tower battlement, lancet windows, buttresses, pitched roof, and trefoil windows of the dormers all suggest the early English Gothic Revival. John de Young was the architect.

The Reverend Benjamin Eaton, a native of Dublin, established Trinity Church and served as its first rector. Charles Hayes wrote in 1879: "He was attracted to Texas by reading a pamphlet or small book that accidentally fell in his hands, which graphically set forth the wonderful resources of this prolific country. On the 16th day of January, 1841, he arrived in Galveston, and at once proceeded to Houston, where he designed [*sic*] locating. He held one service, and preached one sermon, but the accommodations were miserable, the town muddy, and the general appearance so dismal, that he was disenchanted of the beauties of Texas, and turned his face homeward again."[19] While passing through Galveston the second time, Eaton made friends and found the island more agreeable. He began conducting services in temporary quarters, but within 17 months his young parish had erected a church. During the 1842 storm, the church was blown on its side, with a frightened Reverend Eaton inside. The rector escaped through a window with the resolve to build a sturdier house of worship.

Eaton Chapel and Trinity Episcopal Church

Nicholas Clayton designed Eaton Chapel, which was dedicated in 1882, to the south of the church. The chapel shows the complexity of the later Victorian Gothic style. It is also made of red brick, though the exterior has been covered with sandstone mortar. During the same year, Trinity Church was extensively remodeled by architect William H. Tyndall.

A zealous and endearing clergyman, Eaton died in 1871 and was buried in a crypt beneath the chancel of the church.

The 1900 storm brought down the south wall of the Trinity Church. In 1926, the entire church was raised 15 inches above the high water mark of the 1915 storm.

Louis Comfort Tiffany designed the stained glass window, dedicated in 1904, that adorns the west end of the building.

7

GEORGE BALL HOUSE
1857
1405 24th Street

George Ball was senior partner of Ball, Hutchings & Co., which is described in the notes concerning the Hutchings, Sealy Bank Building.

Ball built this large Greek Revival home in 1857. It was originally located at the intersection of 23rd Street and Sealy, now the site of the Rosenberg Library. In 1882, a subsequent owner, Joseph Goldthwaite, made $15,000 worth of additions, including the wing that is now next door at 1401 24th Street. In 1901, John Focke bought the house for $500 at auction with the stipulation that it be moved to make room for the library. Focke moved the house to the site of the then-demolished Texas Cotton Press and divided the structure into the two houses that stand today. The huge Doric columns were cut when the house was moved and the seam is still visible beneath the capitals.

The George Ball House is a good example of

brought to the island to apply gold leaf to interior friezes and medallions.

The house served as headquarters for the Confederate and Union armies during the war. The house was not elevated in the grade raising after the 1900 storm and as a result "lost" several feet of its basement. Similarly, Galveston's grade raising buried the iron fence so that only the uppermost part is visible today. The fence posts, which were raised to the new ground level, indicate the fence's original height.

In 1969, Ashton Villa was scheduled to be razed. Members of the Galveston Historical Foundation spearheaded an effort that saved the building. The house now serves as a museum operated by that organization.

Old Galveston Customs House

later, heavily embellished Greek Revival architecture. The ornate frieze and front entrance architrave are much more elaborate, for example, than the earlier Menard House. The neighborhood that evolved around the Texas Cotton Press property contains approximately 100 Victorian homes, ranging from the splendor of the Ball and Sweeney-Royston houses to modest, raised cottages. This neighborhood is now the Silk Stocking Historic District, protected in 1975 by city ordinance.

9

OLD GALVESTON CUSTOMS HOUSE
1858–61
20th and Postoffice Streets

This handsome, late Greek Revival building was designed as a federal customhouse, courthouse, and post office. The architect was Charles B. Cluskey of Washington, who designed many Neo-classical buildings in Savannah, Georgia. Cluskey and his partner, Edwin W. Moore of Galveston, won the contract for the Customs House from the Treasury Department in 1856. However, because of several years of machinations by the contractors, apparently in an attempt to enhance their fee, construction did not begin in earnest until 1860. By this time, Greek Revival style was passé in much of the country. Nonetheless, the building, in full Greek Revival regalia, must have been an impressive sight in 1861. However, it did not serve the government long, if at all, that year. When results of the statewide secession referendum were tallied on the second day of March, they indicated overwhelming public support for withdrawal from the Union. The customs collector immediately turned over the keys to the customs house to state authorities.[21]

The red brick building forms a rectangle with a large, projecting double gallery facing west and even larger inset galleries facing north and south. Almost all of the detail, including the columns, cornices, balustrades, entablatures, and window architraves, are of cast iron. The ironwork was manufactured in New York and shipped to Galveston. The first-story galleries have Ionic columns, while the second story, greater in height, has Corinthian capitals and a balustrade. The fact that the bricks are not of uniform color suggests that the building was supposed to be painted, as indeed it was for many years. During the 1960s, however, the paint was removed. In 1985, the building will again house the offices of the U.S. Customs Service.

Ashton Villa

8

ASHTON VILLA
1858
2328 Broadway

This was Galveston's first grand departure from Greek Revival. James M. Brown was a New York-born brick mason who journeyed south and grew rich. He manufactured brick, owned a hardware business, and served as president of the Galveston, Houston and Henderson Railroad and the First National Bank of Galveston. Brown, who married the former Rebecca Ashton Stoddard, wanted his home, which he called Ashton Villa, to be a dazzler. He elected to construct one of the earliest Italianate-style residences in Texas.

"In the Civil War decades, the Italianate dwelling preens like the stereotyped Victorian matron—well dressed, well behaved, and self-satisfied. Proportions tend toward the vertical, and ornament toward the florid," observed Carole Rifkind in 1980.[20] But that view is overly harsh. The Italianate structures that have survived have proven to be light, airy buildings, which are very adaptable to modern living without the dark and menacing look of some of the Gothic and Romanesque Victorian creations.

Ashton Villa displayed modern construction techniques as well as style. The fancy window hoods, columns, and fence are of cast iron, which would become very popular after the Civil War. The double gallery, uncommon among Italianate homes, was a concession to the weather and, perhaps, to what we now call the Galveston Style. The brick and plaster were shipped from Philadelphia, the ironwork from England, the hand-carved walnut window valances from Paris. French artisans were

---

10

AUSTIN-FOX HOUSE
CIRCA 1851, 1868–71
1502 Market

Attorney Lorenzo Sherwood, one of the few vocal opponents of slavery at a time when such objections could invite hazard, purchased four lots in 1851 and built his home there. Edward T. Austin, a lawyer and the cousin of Stephen F. Austin, bought the house in 1867 and set about making improvements. The unusual columns, the trim, and the west wing were added during the next several years. More than 70 years later, in 1947, the Fox family acquired the house, less one of the lots.

Austin-Fox House

The setting, with the house set back from the road and surrounded by trees, has the air of a plantation. The present exterior of the house shows that Greek influence endured well into the years of the Victorian heyday. The double gallery and overall balance are Greek, but the ornate gingerbread brackets reveal that the Gothic Revival had reached the island. Large corbels, grouped in pairs, show the influence of the Italianate trim of Ashton Villa. The house embodies the Galveston Style, its design half mindful of local utility and taste and half attuned to the distant rhythms of fashion.

Merchants Mutual Insurance Company Building

11

MERCHANTS MUTUAL INSURANCE COMPANY BUILDING
1870
2317-19 The Strand

A similar building at this site was destroyed by fire in 1869. "This building had the only Mansard roof in the city, and was an ornament of which we were justly proud. Great efforts were made to save it and...it would have been saved, as were some other buildings, had there been iron shutters. It is now almost level with the ground," reported *Flake's Daily Bulletin* after the fire.[22] Architects Donald McKenzie and Fritz Weinherner designed the present copy of the original. Mansard roofs, the rage in the 1870s and 80s, would follow on many Galveston buildings, though few remain today.

12

THOMAS JEFFERSON LEAGUE BUILDING
1871-72
2301-07 The Strand

Nineteenth century Galveston was very vulnerable to fires. Many of the structures were of wood, and the scarcity of land caused buildings to be crowded together. In 1869, a fire was set to cover a robbery at the Moro Castle, an old and popular saloon at The Strand and 23rd Street. The fire quickly spread to neighboring buildings and four city blocks were

destroyed, including the Merchants Mutual Insurance Company Building. Thomas Jefferson League, a lawyer who managed the large real estate empire left by his father, T. M. League, erected this handsome building on the site of the destroyed Moro Castle. There was no architect. It is essentially a plain stuccoed brick facade with cast iron ornaments, including the ground level arcade and window moldings. The original iron cornice has been lost.

Like their counterparts elsewhere, members of the aristocracy of Galveston tended to intermarry, forming a complex web of social connections. A formidable alliance was formed when Thomas Jefferson League married Mary Dorothea Williams, daughter of Samuel May Williams, the banker and merchant. Thomas's brother John Charles League married Nellie Ball, daughter of George Ball, the prominent banker and merchant. John League founded the mainland town of League City, between Galveston and Houston.

Thomas Jefferson League Building

Cast iron facades whose patterns evoked the architectural splendor of Europe were frequently shipped to the hinterlands, where they were applied over a plain exterior. In this case, the iron facade covers only the first story. The ironwork came from George Cronan and Sons of New Orleans.[23]

In 1979, George and Cynthia Mitchell purchased the building and restored it. The League Building is now occupied by a restaurant and several shops.

First Presbyterian Church

13

FIRST PRESBYTERIAN CHURCH
1872-89
1903 Church at 19th Street

When the congregation of First Presbyterian Church elected to replace its wood frame building, the Memphis architectural firm of Jones and Baldwin was commissioned to design the new structure. In 1872, the firm sent a young architect named Nicholas Clayton to Galveston to supervise the construction. Clayton later established his own practice on the island and became Galveston's foremost architect. He designed the Garten Verein Dancing Pavilion, the Bishop's Palace, and the Ashbel Smith Building at the University of Texas Medical Branch. He also designed St. Edward's University and St. Mary's Cathedral, both in Austin.

The congregation had been organized in 1840 by The Reverend John McCullough, who was succeeded by The Reverend Robert Franklin Bunting, a former chaplain for Terry's Texas Rangers in Tennessee during the Civil War. Work on a new chapel began quickly in 1872, but there were many delays.

The chapel, the facade of which faces Church Street at the rear of the present church, was completed in 1876. Subsequent progress on the main church building was so slow it became known as "Bunting's Folly." However, the church was finally finished in 1889, at a cost of $90,000. Architect George E. Dickey designed the interior. In the aftermath of the 1900 storm, the church was used as a temporary mortuary.

First Presbyterian represents the Norman Romanesque Revival style. It is made of brick stuccoed to resemble sandstone. The church facade on 19th Street is flanked by asymmetrical towers, the north with a pyramid roof and the south steeply gabled. The pilasters, stepped wall buttresses, towers, and the pinnacles of the chapel facade all give vertical emphasis to the building. The interior features a handsome stained pine plank ceiling divided by curved pendants. On the plaster above the matching pine wainscoting was a multi-colored stencil of stylized curvilinear design. The stencil has since been covered with fresh plaster. The two center stained glass windows in the north and south walls of the nave were designed by Louis Comfort Tiffany. The artists of the other windows are not known.

Alexander Everett House

14
ALEXANDER EVERETT HOUSE
CIRCA 1873
1211 Church

As with all the Victorian styles, Italianate was subject to the inventive interpretation of its constituents. A particularly energetic derivation is the home of shipbuilder Alexander Barrett Everett.

One of the virtues of Italianate is that it can be easily expanded, unlike the more strictly symmetrical forms of Greek Revival. Everett, the father of eight children, took full advantage of this option. Records indicate several additions. Also, at least one outbuilding, the servants' quarters, appears to have been moved from the rear of the property to adjoin the house.

The playful window and entrance architraves are very unusual, no doubt the improvisation of the carpenter. Altogether, the house is a delightful example of the Victorian mind borrowing from all over the architectural landscape to create something new.

15
HEIDENHEIMER-MARINE BUILDING
1875
21st Street and Ship's Mechanic Row

This no-nonsense Gothic building seems to be imbued with the same solid Teutonic virtues of its namesake, Samson Heindenheimer. The two-story building is of brick, which was covered with a thin layer of cement and embellished with stucco details to resemble stone. Most distinctive of the design is the arcade of ogee, or late medieval, arches on the first floor.

The building seems the antithesis of its soaring, airy neighbor, the Heidenheimer-Hunter Building, also built by Samson, on the west side of the same block. Rather, the Marine Building is squat and assertive in appearance.

Samson Heidenheimer, born in Wurtenberg, Germany, was a very determined entrepreneur. Af-

ter arriving in Galveston about 1858, he worked as a street vendor selling apples. When the Civil War broke out in 1861, Heidenheimer recognized an extraordinary business opportunity. Exempt from military service because he was a German citizen, he engaged in sailing cotton shipments out of Galveston harbor, which required him to elude the Union blockade. By the end of the war, he had realized about $10,000 in profits from his blockade running. Later in his career, he successfully challenged a salt monopoly on the island by purchasing two ships with which to bring salt from Liverpool. Still another monopoly was thwarted by Heidenheimer when he began operating barges to introduce competition in the lighterage trade—the business of partially unloading incoming ships so they could clear the sandbar at the mouth of the harbor.

Heidenheimer erected the Marine Building on a site where he had previously leased a structure for $4,000 per year in gold. The present building cost $15,000 to construct.

Heidenheimer's taste for architecture was further expressed in his home, a four-story, 37-room structure known as Heidenheimer Castle. The castle was destroyed by fire in 1974. One can sense the scale of the home by studying its doors, which now dominate the front of a large contemporary residence at 47 Colony Park Circle in Galveston.

Heidenheimer was an enthusiastic booster of his adopted city. In the Mardi Gras Parade of 1880, he sponsored a wagon drawn by 18 mules. The wagon and the mules were festooned with practical mottos and civic-minded propaganda. Several of the latter dealt with deepening the Galveston Ship Channel, an endeavor that is still an issue today. One of the slogans read, "Texans can do anthing if they pull together." But that spirit did not prevent Galvestonians from chortling with glee when, after one of Heidenheimer's salt barges was caught in a severe rain storm near Houston, a local wag at the *Galveston Daily News* mused, "Houston has a salt water port at last!" Houston had long aspired to build a channel to the Gulf, and of course, the city to the north would have the last laugh. It began dredging in the late 1800s, and eventually created a port that far surpassed Galveston's.

Heidenheimer-Marine Building

Heidenheimer, whose empire included a candy factory, a paper bag business, a cottonseed oil mill, banking interests, and a salt warehouse, died in 1891. He also was a railroad investor, which resulted in his serving as namesake for the town of Heidenheimer in Bell County, Texas.

Because his building was occupied by maritime-related tenants, it later became known as the Marine Building. In 1984, the Heidenheimer-Marine Building was refurbished by George and Cynthia Mitchell to house offices and shops.

16
GARTEN VEREIN DANCING PAVILION
1876
Avenue O and 27th Street

One of the more striking and popular architectural forms of the Victorian period was the octagon. John Maas writes about the eight-sided building: "[It] belongs to the orbit of Orson Squire Fowler and his Octagons. Fowler was a man in the grand and continuing American tradition of spellbinding crackpots. His specialty was phrenology, the pseudo-science of reading character from skull bumps...Fowler did not actually invent the Octagon; there had been polygonal buildings for centuries...He pointed out the undeniable fact that eight walls enclose more space than four walls of the same length and insisted that an octagonal house was the one answer to each and every building problem. Fowler's book *A Home For All, or the Gravel Wall and Octagon Mode of Building, New, Cheap, Convenient, Superior and Adapted to Rich and Poor* was published in 1854. Hundreds of Octagons were built from Maine to California; an exact count of octagonal buildings has been made in New York State—126 are still standing."[24]

Garten Verein Dancing Pavilion

While the octagon poses a number of problems when used as a dwelling, it is well suited for a dancing pavilion. Revelers seated on the perimeter of the huge pavilion are afforded an unobstructed view of the entire ballroom, something a cavernous rectangle could not provide.

The German community in Galveston was large and prosperous. The Garten Verein, or garden club, was one of a number of social clubs for the island's German-speaking citizens. So successful was the club, with its bowling greens, tennis courts, croquet grounds, gardens, and dancing, that it became fashionable even among non-German residents. At some point, membership became open, though only those of German ancestry could own shares. In 1923, the gardens and pavilion were purchased by Stanley Kempner and donated to the city for a public park.

In style, the pavilion is eclectic Victorian, which is to say it defies classification. It was designed by architect Nicholas Clayton. The pilasters with carved capitals, the profuse and flamboyant vergeboard, the expansive use of glass, two balustrades— one of pickets and one of solid panelled wood—and a cupola all work together to produce a stunning, whimsical building.

17
LEMUEL BURR HOUSE
1876
1228 Sealy

This striking house was built by Lemuel C. Burr, a wholesale grocer who came to the island from Belton, Texas. Burr joined the firm of Kauffman and Runge, a large trading company dealing in groceries and cotton. The firm established the first direct coffee trade between Texas and South America. In 1883, Burr sold his residence to his employer, Julius Kauffman, Jr., for $11,500. Kauffman's business activities are described in the notes on the Kauffman and Runge Building, built in 1881–82. Title to the house passed from the Kauffman family to Captain James P. Alvey in 1890. Alvey, who had served as an officer under General Stonewall Jackson in the Civil War and fought in the Battle of Gettysburg, was active in banking and real estate in Galveston. The captain was married to the former Jennie McCullough, daughter of First Presbyterian Church founder John McCullough.

Similarities between the Burr House and other homes by Nicholas Clayton suggest that the prolific architect might have designed this structure as well. Clearly, a skilled hand was at work here. Many features distinguish the house—the richly detailed cornice, the paired brackets, the graceful arches of

the double gallery—but it is the balance and harmony of these elements that make it such a successful composition. The window architraves are particularly outstanding, with a peaked shape that reflects the the lofty pediment above and a Lone Star of Texas motif applied to the moldings. The arch below the broken pediment of the front facade seems designed to catch the prevailing southeasterly breezes.

18

MARX AND KEMPNER BUILDINGS
1877–78
2117-19 The Strand

The original buildings on these lots were destroyed in a large fire, the "great conflagration of 1877." The east building was erected by partners Marx Marx and Harris Kempner, Galveston liquor and cigar wholesalers. After the fire, the business moved elsewhere on The Strand, and the present structure was rebuilt for new tenants, including a candy manufacturer. Oscar Springer, a subsequent owner, published *Die Galveston Post,* a German newspaper, among other interests. The original ironwork on the building was removed during the repair of hurricane damage in the 1930s, and the brick building was left with a smooth stucco facade.[25]

Kempner and his offspring went on to accumulate significant holdings in banking, land, the cotton trade, and sugar refining. The family still controls the Imperial Sugar Company of Sugarland, Texas.

Clara Lang had the west building constructed of brick with artificial stone trim. It was later acquired by Oscar Springer and incorporated into his building next door. The orginal fourth floor was lost in the 1915 hurricane.

In 1976, a bicentennial grant from the City of Galveston was used to pay for the present mural that adorns the facade of both buildings. Richard Haas, a New York muralist who did much to renew interest in *trompe l'oeil,* or "fool the eye," paintings, designed and executed the mural. Haas studied the drawings of Nicholas Clayton and borrowed details from buildings all over the city for his painting, which most passersby mistake for actual architectural detail. Artist Margaret Rochelle designed the handsome stencil applied to the floor of the second-story hall.

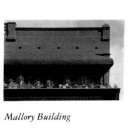

Mallory Building

*First National Bank
Building*

19

FIRST NATIONAL BANK BUILDING
1877
2127 The Strand

The original three-story building here was lost to the 1877 fire. This two-story replacement was designed by architect P. M. Comegys. Some of the ironwork of the original building may have been used in the present structure. In any event, the metal ornamentation is rich in detail. The sidewalk of contrasting tiles was brought from England.

Of the iron-front buildings that have survived in Galveston, none has a complete iron facade. Most often, they possess an iron first-story facade and cornice, with metal window moldings for the second and third stories. The full facades must have been impressive. "These great iron fronts, fitted like picture frames two and three stories high, over the faces of brick and frame buildings, were accepted during the late fifties in Galveston as a prime sign of progress...In 1858, the Chamber of Commerce, under the direction of Joseph Kauffman, inaugurated a vigorous campaign to put an iron front on every store in the city."[26]

*Robert B. Garnett
House*

20

ROBERT B. GARNETT HOUSE
1877–79
3518 Avenue M

The Garnett House, an example of the Italianate style executed in wood, was built by Robert Garnett, a carpenter, builder, and cistern maker. In making his own residence, Garnett seemed intent on showing off the handiwork of his trade. The ornately-carved details of the brackets of the entablature, the entrance, and the bay windows are among the best examples of vernacular craftsmanship on the island. The formidable double storm doors fold inward to form vestibule paneling.

An American eagle decorates the bronze front doorknobs. The house has six slate fireplaces and an impressive staircase whose bannister sweeps upstairs and then doubles back to form the railing for the large second-story landing.

Garnett left the island in 1899. By 1974, the house had changed hands several times and fallen into disrepair. It was then purchased and restored to its former elegance by Latané Temple, grandson of the founder of the Temple lumber interests. The house changed hands twice more, and the current owner has painted the structure in a polychrome scheme to accentuate the detailed wood trim.

21

MALLORY BUILDING
1878
2110-12 The Strand

To the contemporary eye the ornate buildings of The Strand are so impressive that it is hard to imagine that the majority of these were originally occupied by wholesale businesses. Before the grade raising of 1904–10, the thresholds on this busy street were three or four feet off the ground, so that wagons could more easily be unloaded. Nineteenth century photographs of The Strand show that, in spite of the fancy architecture, the sidewalks were strewn with barrels and boxes, drays were parked everywhere, idle horses were tied to the gallery columns, and laborers were constantly loading and unloading freight. Most of the large wholesale houses were devoted to acquiring and storing goods shipped from the East for resale to inland Texas merchants.

The Mallory Building still has the look of a "working" building. The first-story arcade and the curved metal awning of the second story give the building a simple, utilitarian appearance. Almost all the buildings on The Strand once had similar sidewalk canopies.

David D. Mallory erected this building in 1878. It replaced the original Mallory Building, which was destroyed in Galveston's 1877 fire. Another fire, in 1881, gutted the building, and it was rebuilt again by 1882. Mallory, who operated a provisioning firm and general store, was the son of Charles H. Mallory, who founded the Mallory Steamship Line. For much of the 20th century, the building housed several produce companies. Hence the cornice reads, "Produce Bldg." Advertisements for Focke, Wilkens and Lange, a wholesale grocery firm located in the building in 1882, show that a triangular pediment once stood over the cornice.

Bill H. Fullen purchased the building in 1972 and became one of the pioneers of the movement to revive The Strand. His store and restaurant, The Old Strand Emporium, which opened in the building in 1974, operate there today.

*Leon & H. Blum Building
(The Tremont House)*

22

LEON & H. BLUM BUILDING
(THE TREMONT HOUSE)
1879–80, 1882
2300 Ship's Mechanic Row

Houston architect Eugene T. Heiner designed this large three-story brick structure for the wholesale dry goods firm of Leon & H. Blum. The west part of the building was completed in 1880, and a large addition to the east was added two years later.

Leon Blum was born in Alsace in 1836. He came

to America in 1852 and joined his brother, a merchant, in Texas. Shortly before the Civil War, the two moved to Galveston. To avoid the Union blockade, they established their business in Matamoras, Mexico, during the war. When the company was reorganized in 1869, five Blums were involved. The firm was named Leon & H. Blum, with the initial referring to Leon's cousin, Hyman.[27]

The company became one of the largest wholesale firms in the South, with annual sales of approximately $5 million in 1885. It had offices in New York, Boston, and Paris and employed numerous warehouse workers, 95 office clerks, and a roving sales force of 30. Leon Blum earned the moniker "The Merchant Prince" during the company's prosperous years. A depression in the 1890s crippled the wholesale business, which failed in 1896. Thereafter, Blum was involved in shipping, railroads, and land sales until his death in 1906. The building later housed a department store, The *Galveston Tribune,* and several other businesses. In 1984, the building was restored and converted into a hotel, The Tremont House, by George and Cynthia Mitchell.

At one time the Blum Building included a steep Mansard roof with iron cresting. As a part of the restoration, a Mansard roof with dormers has been added to form the hotel's fourth story. The building's architect, Eugene Heiner, also designed the Kauffman & Runge Building in Galveston and the Cotton Exchange Building in Houston.

Kauffman & Runge Building

23

KAUFFMAN & RUNGE BUILDING
1881–82
22nd Street and Ship's Mechanic Row

The firm of Kauffman & Runge descended from a trading house founded by Julius Kauffman in 1842. His partner was Henry Runge, a native of Bremen, Germany, who had been in business in Indianola, Texas. Indianola was repeatedly struck by severe storms, causing Runge to abandon it for Galveston in 1866.

An 1887 survey of commerce in Galveston said of Kauffman & Runge, "For many years, it has been the largest cotton exporting house here."[28] By this time, Kauffman had been succeeded by his son, Julius Jr., and Runge by his nephew, Julius Runge. Evidently the members of the second generation were intrepid. For 10 days in 1884 the firm orchestrated a bid to corner the world cotton market, an unsuccessful and costly maneuver. Prior to this speculation, Runge the younger had been president of both the Galveston Cotton Exchange and First National Bank.[29]

The firm of Kauffman & Runge used its ties to Germany to establish a brisk cotton trade with that country. The principals were so fond of the United States that they encouraged others to cross the Atlantic. As agents for the North German Lloyds Line, they brought hundreds of Germans from Bremen to Galveston.

The building was designed by Eugene Heiner, an American architect trained in Europe. White stone work and several colors of brick originally gave the building a polychrome effect. As a part of a 1976 restoration, the brick was painted to regain the polychrome detailing, and the cornice, lost in the 1900 storm, was rebuilt.

Maco Stewart, Sr., bought the building in 1905. Three years later, he founded the Stewart Title Company, which is now a large, Houston-based title insurance firm doing business nationwide. The company is still the main tenant, and the four-story red structure is often called the Stewart Title Building.

Trueheart-Adriance Building

24

TRUEHEART-ADRIANCE BUILDING
1881
212 22nd Street

While the Kauffman & Runge Building uses more than one color of brick to create added interest, the best example of polychromal brick architecture on the island is this three-story building constructed for one of the oldest real estate firms in Texas. An early principal in the firm, founded in 1857, was H. M. Trueheart. John Adriance joined the company later.

The building is pure Victorian, a combination of Corinthian capitals, Greek pediment and dentils, Romanesque third-story windows, and many other flourishes. The bell-shaped curves in the upper sashes of the ground floor windows are unusual. Nicholas Clayton used a crazy quilt of motifs to create this energetic and polished office building.

H. M. Trueheart served as provost-marshall after Union troops were driven from the city during the Battle of Galveston on New Year's Day, 1863. One of his earliest tasks was to draft every fit, white male inhabitant between the ages of 18 and 40 into military service. Evidently not everyone was eager to enlist. In order to discourage men from eluding the patrols, Trueheart issued a warning that, "guards are ordered to fire upon any person…who shall attempt to escape, by running or otherwise." That ended the provost-marshall's conscription difficulties.

25

GREENLEVE, BLOCK & COMPANY BUILDING
1882
2310-14 The Strand

Nicholas Clayton designed this building with the intention of distinguishing it from the many iron-front structures already lining The Strand. The typical iron facades were ordered from a catalog and contained an admixture of Victorian themes. Because the buildings they covered were essentially of smooth brick, the iron facades were of necessity flat and somewhat two-dimensional. Clayton, on the other hand, created a building much richer in texture. Three bays on either side of the front elevation project out, providing the standard sidewalk arcade. But the six middle bays are recessed.

The columns are the best example of Clayton's ability to make the iron front more three-dimensional. They stand out well in front of the facade, attached only by a lacy iron trellis. The inner columns, which support the brick facade of the upper stories, also serve to make the iron front more convincing.

The building was erected for Greenleve, Block and Company, a wholesale dry goods business. The initials of the firm's principals, Abraham Greenleve, Louis Block, Louis Michael, and Leopold Oppenheimer, appear in the shields above the second story. Two years after construction of the building in 1882, the firm reorganized as Block, Oppenheimer & Company.

Greenleve, Block & Company Building

The iron facade and an elaborate cornice were cast by a Galveston foundry. The cornice was lost to the 1900 storm, and the original fourth story was removed by a ship chandlers supply firm that occupied the building for many years.[30] The iron and stuccoed brick building is one of the most handsome on The Strand, though, sadly, it looks "beheaded" without its cornice and top floor.

Mensing Brothers Building

26
MENSING BROTHERS BUILDING
1882
2118-28 The Strand

The brothers Gustave and William Mensing, who had come to Galveston in 1868, established a cotton factoring firm in 1873. By 1882, the company had prospered sufficiently to build this large, two-story building. Cotton auctions were conducted in one of the second-story rooms. In this structure, as in the Greenleve, Block & Company Building, one can see the more complex work of masons who fashioned stucco details over the brick. This is not the simple scoring of the stucco to resemble stone, but rather a complete array of arches, window moldings, and column capitals.

27
W. L. MOODY BUILDING
1884
2202-06 The Strand

William L. Moody came to Texas from Virginia in 1852. Having attended the University of Virginia, where he studied law, he quickly established a law practice in Fairfield, though he soon gave it up to become a merchant. Moody fought for the South in the Civil War and retired from service as colonel. After the war, he moved to Galveston, where he started a commission and cotton factoring house.

Colonel Moody was joined in business by his son, W. L. Moody, Jr., who succeeded in expanding the family business and creating one of the largest fortunes in the United States. The younger Moody wrote that, before the wharf area was improved, the rear of this building extended into the

W. L. Moody Building

water. He was thus "able to catch fish from the rear windows of the building."[31]

Nicholas Clayton designed the structure, which was originally four stories, with large elaborate pediments and a cornice topped with fancy clocks. The 1900 storm ripped off the cornice and fourth story, leaving a humbler building in its wake. The first level has unusual iron columns that are partially fluted and partially cast with a lattice-style pattern.

W. L. Moody, Jr., left an immense empire that lives on today in various entities. He founded American National Insurance Company, the second-largest insurance company in Texas, which was first housed in the Moody Building. The company today occupies the 20-story building at One Moody Plaza that dominates the island skyline. The Moody Foundation, whose assets of more than $280 million are used to support a variety of worthy philanthropic endeavors, including historic preservation in Galveston, was created by Moody and his wife, the former Libby Rice Shearn.

Sweeney-Royston House

28
SWEENEY-ROYSTON HOUSE
1885
2402 Avenue L

James M. Brown, the entrepreneur who built Ashton Villa, presented this house, complete with furnishings, to his daughter Matilda as a wedding gift. Brown located her honeymoon cottage just around the corner from his own home, and, in what may have been an act of prescience, deeded it to her as separate property. The groom was Thomas Sweeney, who was in the shipping business.

Looking at the house, one wonders if Brown ordered a standard one-and-a-half story cottage and then got carried away! Surely the expense of adding the ornate trim, stained glass, and interior details was significant enough to have justified the construction of a larger, more pretentious home. In any event, the outcome was a fanciful and richly appointed Victorian cottage.

Some anecdotal evidence suggests that Nicholas Clayton designed this house, though there is no mention of it among Clayton's papers. One obvious theme is the mariner's wheel motif of the gallery balustrade, no doubt an allusion to Sweeney's occupation. Another is the ingenious repetition of triangles throughout the house. The gables include three triangular pediments, to the front and on both sides. The windows of the gables project forward, forming triangular bays. Another triangular pediment is mounted above the central bay of the gallery. The bay window of the east side supports a small balcony from the east gable. A large, zinc molding, pierced with a curvilinear design, crowns the roof deck. The house originally had a tricolor roof of scallop-shaped slates. The slates remain on some of the gables and on the rear tower.

A jewelled and stained-glass window pierces the chimney of the second parlor fireplace. Mahogany, curly pine, and long leaf pine are handsomely worked in the cabinets and interior wood work. The 10-foot cypress storm doors have rosette windows of jewelled glass.

The house was not elevated for the grade raising, though the basement was maintained. The stuccoed brick arches of the foundation originally included large windows for what is now the basement. Before the city water system was installed, rainwater was collected from the roof and stored in the cement cistern, 16 feet in diameter and 8 feet deep, that remains in the basement. Though the house appears small, the interior floor space measures 3,500 square feet.

After the birth of their third child, Thomas and Matilda Sweeney were divorced, and the house was unoccupied for several years. In 1911, attorney Mart H. Royston purchased the house and lived there for 43 years. He founded the firm of Royston and Rayzor, a large admiralty law firm still active in Houston and Galveston as Royston, Rayzor, Vickery & Williams.

John Hutchings House

29

JOHN HUTCHINGS HOUSE
1856, 1885–88
2816 Avenue O

Robert Mills, a wealthy planter, cotton trader, and banker, built a two-story house here in 1856 for his niece, Minnie Knox, and her new husband, John Henry Hutchings. The house was damaged in 1885, after which Nicholas Clayton was hired to rebuild and expand the structure. The mansion that resulted has some Neo-Classical details, but is largely an eclectic design. Clayton had the brick exterior stuccoed with concrete and added a third floor, portico, and front gallery. The adaptation obviously posed problems, and the house turned out rather awkward. Whatever effect the grand south portico achieves is spoiled by the odd collection of shapes overhead. The asymmetrical and busy roofline and the squat, heavy columns of the third-story gallery seem out of place. Most likely, Clayton was not given a free hand. He is said to have referred to his remodelling work here as "frilling." The architect had much more success with the interesting Romanesque carriage house east of the main building. Within two years of the construction of the carriage house, more remodelling took place. It is uncertain whether Clayton was involved in that work.

Hutchings, whose business activities are described in the notes concerning the Hutchings Sealy Bank Building, died in 1906.

About 1890, Hutching's youngest daughter, Rey Hutchings Belknap, oversaw further changes to the house in preparation for her debut. At this time, a ballroom, two stories tall and crowned by a stained wood vaulted ceiling, was added to the third floor. Mrs. Belknap became a patroness of scholarly publishing. She survived her son, Waldron Phoenix Belknap, Jr., who founded the Belknap Press at Harvard University. When she died at age 86 in 1959, she left the greatest part of her estate to the Belknap Press, which earned her a place in the annals of scholarship, but the ire of some of her Galveston relatives.

An iron fence surrounds the sprawling grounds, which contain a greenhouse for the current lady of the house, who is an orchid enthusiast. The mansion has remained in the Hutchings family.

Jacob Sonnentheil House

30

JACOB SONNENTHEIL HOUSE
1886–88
1826 Sealy Avenue

Plenty of Carpenter Gothic houses exist around the country, but few, if any, can rival the incredible exuberance of the Sonnentheil House. Here is the Gothic Revival interpreted in wood. In addition, the house borrows freely from the French Second Empire, Greek, and Italianate styles.

The gallery is supported by three different types of columns. Carved heads, each representing a different European nationality, adorn the pilasters of the second story's south bay window. Light and shadow play across the broad porches as the intricate trellis work filters the rays of the sun. Rich detail can be found everywhere.

Jacob Sonnentheil was in the dry goods business. In 1884, he joined the firm of Block, Oppenheimer & Co., whose commercial building is described elsewhere. Though his new concern was one of the largest wholesalers in the city, the company was soon in financial trouble. For years local lore concluded that the expense of his new house caused Sonnentheil's downfall. His company did indeed fail in 1887. But shortly thereafter, the *Galveston Daily News* reported the construction of "a frame dwelling" at this address that cost $14,000, a sizeable expense for a man in financial distress. Sonnentheil appears to have recovered in any case. He was later active in the vinegar, pickle, and insurance businesses.

He died in 1908 while on vacation in New York. The *New York Times* reported that Sonnentheil, a native of Bavaria, was "one of the very few Germans to fight through the Civil War with the Confederate Army."

Evidence suggests that Nicholas Clayton designed the house, but this cannot be confirmed. A shelf board in the pantry was discovered to have the message "1887 Ducie" painted on its underside. This could be the hidden signature of Daniel Winters Ducie, Clayton's gifted carpenter. Also, the floor plan of the house is very similar to other Clayton designs.

31

TEMPLE B'NAI ISRAEL
1870, 1887
816 22nd Street

Architect Fred Stewart designed this odd building in 1870, though significant additions were handled by Nicholas Clayton in 1887. The result is a curious blend of East and West. The Gothic can be seen in the windows and buttresses of the nave on the south elevation. A huge, Gothic stained-glass window once filled the arch that dominates the west facade, but it has been replaced with ludicrous aluminum frame windows. A Moorish influence is evident in the arches above the windows and doors of the west side, some of the shapes of which are repeated in the Moorish-inspired design of Sacred Heart Church of 1903-04. There were also four Oriental-looking minarets flanking the pediment of the west facade. Shorn of its lofty minarets, and with most of its windows plugged, the present building bears little resemblance to the original structure. The congregation sold the building in 1953. It is now a Masonic Temple.

Walter Gresham House
(The Bishop's Palace)

32

WALTER GRESHAM HOUSE (THE BISHOP'S PALACE)
1887–93
1402 Broadway

In Walter Gresham, Nicholas Clayton had the client of an architect's dreams. Gresham provided the freedom, the budget, the materials, and the time for Clayton to create this *tour de force*.

The house is an extreme example of the exuberance of late Victorian taste in America. In 1961, the Gresham House was listed among the 100 important American structures built between 1861–1961 that were compiled for the centennial of the American Institute of Architects. Romanesque, Queen Anne, Renaissance, Chateauesque—all receive homage in the house. A legion of stonecutters and carpenters spent six years building the palace. Though Gresham told the newspapers the house

would cost $75,000, the actual cost was probably between $250,000 and $500,000.

Walter Gresham was born in Virginia in 1841 to a family of well-to-do lawyers and planters. He earned a law degree from the University of Virginia and fought with Lee's Rangers in the Army of Virginia during the Civil War. With his family's fortune gone as a result of the hostilities, Gresham travelled to Galveston in 1866. The young attorney, who arrived with five dollars to his name, promptly established a law practice and became involved in the railroads. Gresham and a group of other Galvestonians acquired the Gulf, Colorado and Santa Fe Company. He also served in the Texas legislature and the U.S. Congress. In 1887, he commissioned Nicholas Clayton to build the grandest mansion in Texas, and the home was formally opened on New Year's Day, 1893.

The three-story mansion, mounted on a partially raised basement, is of limestone, granite, and red sandstone. The roof includes several styles of glazed tile. Numerous towers, gables, and chimneys provide a busy and irregular roof line. Adding further interest and height are the stone finials and the cast iron griffins and dragons at the roof apexes. The balustrades of the first and second-story galleries and the third-story balconies are of cast iron. On the east side, an apse-shaped glass conservatory was built for Mrs. Gresham's plants.

In 1923, the Galveston-Houston Diocese of the Roman Catholic Church bought the home for $40,500. The house then became the bishop's residence, and it has since been known as the Bishop's Palace. In 1963, the diocese opened the house as a museum.

Landes House

33

LANDES HOUSE
1887
1604 Postoffice Street

H. A. Landes was a well-to-do wholesaler, cotton broker, and shipper who owned his own fleet. He built this large, brick Romanesque home for $30,000 in 1887. Because he was in the shipping business, Landes was relatively free of geographic constraints when it came to obtaining building materials and furnishings. The wood in the hallway, drawing room, music room, dining room, and stairway is solid cherry that was brought to the island as ballast in his ships. The leather trim and panels inside the house and the handsome exterior tiles are from Spain. To embellish the leather, Landes is said to have brought Spanish artisans to the island.

The Landes House, designed by the Houston firm of Dickey & Helmich, comprises a procession of striking architectural elements. A turret on the south elevation features a Mansard roof, while near it, a small, false turret is solid masonry. The house has elaborate terra-cotta cornices and, on the double gallery, has a series of double columns, connected with fancy ironwork that surpasses in detail the more common wood gingerbread.

Originally, a door at the top of the tower enabled Landes to watch his ships in port. The large gable was initially crowned by three small turrets, lost to a storm years ago.

Landes's wife was related to the family of Walter Gresham, who built the house now called the Bishop's Palace at the same time the Landes House was under construction. A curious interior feature, the placement off the hallway of a folding lavatory taken from a railway car, seems to have impressed both families. Both houses have this forerunner of the "wet bar."

From the Landes family, the house passed to John P. McDonough, who spent some 50 years here. Later, the structure was given to the Dominican order of nuns, who used it for a school. The house was acquired by the present owner in 1969, and its restoration continues to this day. Intricate ironwork was remade for the gallery using 19th century techniques in 1983, and it is scheduled for installation in 1985. The cistern now in the yard, which was a beer vat acquired from a brewery, replaced a copper cistern located on the roof and given to the war effort in the 1940s.

While the Landes House possesses a burdensome countenance, with its dark red color and monumental scale, its character is leavened by the graceful ironwork and the delicately patterned tile over the windows. One of the oddest houses on the island, it tends either to charm or appall its beholder. Among the virtues of the design is its durability. Though damaged in the storms of 1943 and 1983, the house remains a sturdy fortress. A portrait of Landes is carved in the left front door.

Frederick Beissner House

34
FREDERICK BEISSNER HOUSE
1887
1702 Ball

William H. Roystone designed this flamboyant house for Frederick W. Beissner in 1887. Beissner was the son of a prominent local hotelier, Charles Ludwig Beissner, who had left Bremen, Germany, for Galveston in 1842. The elder Beissner opened the Washington Hotel at 21st Street and Avenue C, which preceded the 1873 hotel of the same name that burned in 1983.[32]

Frederick was a clerk at J. D. Skinner & Son, a cotton firm located on The Strand, when the house was built. He was later in the real estate business. In 1914, the home was purchased by Henry Toujouse, a wine and liquor importer. He operated the well-known Toujouse Saloon in his Stag Hotel downtown. The enormous mahogany bar from the saloon is now located in the Toujouse Bar at the Tremont House hotel in the Leon & H. Blum Building.

In the Beissner House, Roystone produced a structure that faces the corner, yet has outstanding facades for both the Ball and 17th Street exposures. In this way, both streets get equal treatment, and neither is relegated to a "side" view of the residence. The house is essentially two wings built at a 90-degree angle. At the vertex of the angle on the second story is a square section with its own gabled roof and distinct cornice. On the first story, this space is pentagonal and forms a large entrance hall. Both levels are surrounded by galleries.

The most arresting feature of the house is the floral motif of the exterior trim. Flower shapes pierce the arches of the gallery and appear in the gable ends and gallery railings. As the eye moves over the rich millwork, flowers seem to peek out from every nook. To add further interest, the designer used a variety of textures for the siding. Shingles cut and applied in three patterns—fish scale, square, and wavy—form a descending progression to a base of standard overlapping wood

siding. Somehow, all this architectural commotion binds together to form a striking composition.

George Sealy House (The Open Gates)

35
GEORGE SEALY HOUSE (THE OPEN GATES)
1887–89
2424 Broadway

This large, neo-Renaissance mansion was built by prominent merchant and banker George Sealy. He was extremely successful, had a large family, and—perhaps most important in terms of the nature of this house—a wife who was accustomed to grand living. Magnolia Willis Sealy had enjoyed the comforts of her mother's impressive house at Tremont and Broadway and her sister's Greek Revival mansion located on the present site of the Rosenberg Library. (The latter house is described elsewhere as the George Ball House.)

In order to build his bride something comparable, Sealy dispatched her to New York in 1886 to hire "the finest architect in the country." Mrs. Sealy performed her errand well, securing the services of Stanford White of the celebrated firm of McKim, Mead & White. Sealy purchased a large lot on fashionable Broadway at 25th Street, only two blocks from his mother-in-law's residence. A large home, some cavalry barracks, and a huge pine tree were razed to make room for White's creation. Construction began in 1887 and ended in 1889. Galveston architect Nicholas Clayton, whose ego was no doubt bruised when he did not get the commission himself, served as supervising architect for the construction. Clayton was able to make a statement only with the carriage house, which he designed. Romanesque in style, the carriage house, built in 1891, is much warmer and more accessible than White's forbidding palace.

Margaret Sealy Burton, Sealy's daughter, reflected on the safety of her huge home during the 1900 storm, writing: "As people were swept in the turbulent waters they were pulled into the boats by the sailors who had their boats tied to our fence, and a large number of people were saved by others who were standing on our porch upstairs. They grabbed them by the hair or any place they could hold to and pulled them up to the porch…the house was filled all day and night with over 400 people who came there for safety, or who had been rescued from a watery grave….There was 15 feet of seawater (in the basement) which reached the beautifully polished oak floors above."

A partner in Hutchings, Sealy & Co., Sealy was also active in the Gulf, Colorado and Santa Fe Railroad, Texas Guarantee and Trust Co., the Galveston Wharf Co., the Galveston Cotton Exchange, Bluefields Banana Co., Southern Cotton Compress Co., and many other ventures. He died on a New York-bound train in 1901, while on his way to arrange financing for Galveston's recovery from the great storm. The Sealy family later gave the Open Gates to the University of Texas Medical Branch, which now uses it as a conference center.

36
JOHN DARRAGH HOUSE
1888–89
519 15th Street

A common practice in 19th century Galveston was the joining of two or more existing structures to

*Ashbel Smith Building
(Old Red)*

*John Darragh
House*

form a single, more impressive house. The home of John L. Darragh, once president of the Galveston Wharf Company, exemplifies this method, which can also be seen in the Alexander Everett House and many others about the city. Standing from some distance away, one can see the roof lines of the two original structures converging between the cupola and the flat deck of the roof. Darragh could watch the progress of ships in the harbor from the high cupola. The two towers suggest Queen Anne influence, while the columns are derived from the Classical orders. The original houses are fairly spare, but the towers are dripping in Victorian trim—brackets, curlicues, fan-shaped windows, panels, fish-scale shingles. The architect for the project was Alfred Muller, who also designed the iron fence, itself an amazing tangle of shapes.

In spite of its contradictions, the house succeeds at being the wood palace that John Darragh envisioned. It is imbued with that foible so keenly Victorian, and yet so present in any contemporary suburb, the pursuit of grandeur. The Darragh house is also one of the saddest buildings in Galveston. At present it lies vacant, deteriorating with each day of neglect.

McDonald House

38

ASHBEL SMITH BUILDING (OLD RED)
1890
914-16 The Strand

In 1873, Dr. Ashbel Smith, who had been surgeon general of the Republic of Texas, reorganized the Galveston Medical College. The Texas Medical College, as the new school was called, later became the medical branch of the University of Texas. In 1889, the state paid for Nicholas Clayton to visit several medical college buildings in other states, including those of Johns Hopkins, the University of Pennsylvania, Harvard, and the College of Physicians and Surgeons in New York. Clayton then submitted plans for a three-story Romanesque building with round towers at each end and an octagonal central tower. Unlike prevailing Romanesque fashion, the building is symmetrical. The 1900 storm cost the school its towers, as well as the spires on each of the six remaining column-like towers of the front elevation. The storm actually had a moderating influence on what was a rather gaudy building.

The brickwork is particularly detailed, creating several different textures. The carved, red sandstone columns of the entrance include a Lone Star motif.

The Ashbel Smith Building, which was restored in 1984, is still in use by the University of Texas Medical Branch. Students and faculty often call it by its nickname, "Old Red."

*John Clement Trube
House*

37

McDONALD HOUSE
1889 or 1890
926 Winnie

Liberty S. McKinney, a wholesale grocer, built this richly carved wood house in either 1889 or 1890. He and several friends rode out the 1900 storm here. In about 1905, D. D. McDonald, a lawyer, acquired the house. He replaced the 14 live oak trees that had lined the south and west sides of the property before the storm. Hence the existing trees are more than 80 years old.

The iron fence was manufactured in Springfield, Ohio. An 1894 photograph shows an ornate cast-iron railing around the widow's walk. That railing, along with a colorful, geometrically patterned slate roof, are gone. Within the arches between the turned columns of the galleries are mariner's wheel details similar to those of the Sweeney-Royston House. The 11-foot double storm doors are carved of cypress. The inner doors have engraved ruby glass over clear glass panels.

39

JOHN CLEMENT TRUBE HOUSE
1890
1627 Sealy

"...this is the strangest house in a city of strange houses," wrote architect Howard Barnstone in *The Galveston That Was.*

John Trube was a gardener for a nobleman in his homeland of Denmark. After acquiring substantial wealth through a real estate business in the New World, Trube chose to toast his success by erecting a building inspired by a landmark from the Old World. The present owners, Trube's descendants, report that the home was based on a castle in Kiel. Alfred Muller, a Galveston architect, designed the house, which was built at a cost of $9,700.

A battlement tower stands guard over the house

on the north side. An 1894 photograph shows that the tower once had a fancy iron railing. The house's gray slate mansard roof has nine gables. The exterior is brick covered with stucco and rusticated to look like stone. The west chimney is bisected by a stained-glass window. The burning torches atop the original iron fence posts are repeated in the details of the tower bastions, and the torch motif reappears in the pressed metal ceiling of the foyer. The house is rich in stained-glass windows.

Muller, a contemporary of Nicholas Clayton, also designed Old City Hall and the Darragh House.

Raised Cottage at 2008 Avenue N½

40
RAISED COTTAGE
CIRCA 1894
2008 Avenue N½

Galveston has hundreds of raised cottages with gingerbread ornamentation. Improvised by the carpenters who built them, the cottages often possess a charming originality in spite of their numbers.

This cottage was built for August J. Henck, a real estate agent and commissioner of deeds. Henck lived on the more fashionable Sealy Street, or Avenue I, and the cottage appears to have been a rental property. Records indicate that the house was usually occupied by his relatives, most of whom worked in Henck's office at the Washington Hotel.

The arches of the front gallery have elaborate pierced spandrels. An applied-wood sunburst, fish-scale shingles, and scroll-work corbels dress up the front gable.

Joel B. Wolfe House

41
JOEL B. WOLFE HOUSE
CIRCA 1894
1602 Ball

The asymmetry and soft curves of this house suggest the influence of the Queen Anne style, but with a strong eclectic flair. Some of the house's many owners have called it *Maison des Fleurs,* which is appropriate, considering that the design seems dedicated to flowers. Four-petal flower trim is repeated in the frieze and the tower. Larger stylized flowers are incorporated in the balustrade of the second story. More flora appear in the gable ends and architraves over the windows. The flower motif continues inside on the wainscoting and the ceilings.

Joel B. Wolfe built the house around 1894. Wolfe and his brother sold machinery, including engines, boilers, and cotton gins.

Few remaining homes in Galveston possess such a collection of applied-wood gingerbread, formed by attaching two or more pieces of millwork together

to achieve greater relief. Another example of this style is the Frederick Beissner House, one block west.

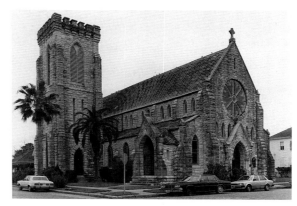

Grace Episcopal Church

42
GRACE EPISCOPAL CHURCH
1894–95
1115 36th Street at Avenue L

During the 1870s, membership of Trinity Episcopal Church grew to such an extent that a Sunday school was formed to serve the west end of the parish. At 36th Street and Avenue L, a small frame Gothic church was built in 1874 and called Trinity Chapel. Two years later, an independent parish was formed here, and the chapel became Grace Church. In 1884, Mr. and Mrs. Henry Rosenberg, long active in Trinity Church, transferred to the new parish. A native of Switzerland, Rosenberg was a successful merchant with interests in banking, railroads, and the Galveston Wharf Company. He also had wide philanthropic interests, the most visible reminders of which are the Rosenberg Library and the monument to the heroes of the Texas Revolution, at Broadway and Rosenberg Avenue. When Rosenberg died in 1893, he left $30,000 for a new church building.

Nicholas Clayton was hired to design the new Grace Church. He built a Gothic Revival structure of white limestone. The straightforward design includes many of the elements of the Victorian Gothic, including gable entrances, a crennelated tower, buttresses, and lancet and rose windows. Rosenberg's widow closely monitored the construction and provided an additional $10,000 for interior furnishings. The woodwork, much of it handcarved in Switzerland, is outstanding.

The parish grew to 220 by 1895, but nearly half of its congregation was killed in the 1900 storm. Grace Church was raised four and a half feet during the ensuing grade raising, at a cost of $7,000. Membership declined further, particularly as a result of the 1915 storm and World War I, and in 1923, Grace Church was returned to mission status. It was reorganized as full parish with a resident rector in 1944.

Grand Opera House

43
GRAND OPERA HOUSE
1894
2012-20 Postoffice Street

By the early 1890s, the opera house in Galveston had become overcrowded, and entertainment magnate Henry Greenwall threatened to eliminate the island from his theatrical circuit if improved facilities were not provided. Leading businessmen such as

Leon Blum and John and George Sealy responded quickly by purchasing stock in a new opera house venture. Curiously, the Grand Opera House was constructed parallel to and behind the Hotel Grand, the length of which fronts Postoffice Street. The two buildings are joined only at the main entrance. A five-foot air space originally divided the hotel and auditorium.

Frank Cox, a New Orleans architect, designed the complex. The Hotel Grand is a four-story building that once had a one-story mansard tower over the entrance. The brick structure, trimmed in stone with terra-cotta ornaments, was completed in late 1894 at a cost of $67,550. Romanesque in style, it has a large semicircular arch at the main entrance. The hotel offices, a restaurant, and stores occupied the first level of the hotel building, with 75 rooms located on the upper three floors. The opera house seated nearly 1,500 and was one of the earliest such theaters to be designed using modern theories of acoustics. Both gas and electric lighting systems were installed, and there were separate furnaces for the auditorium and stage.

The opera house staged melodrama, opera, musical comedy, plays, and concert artists. Among the many luminaries to perform there were George M. Cohan, James O'Neill, John Barrymore, Isadora Duncan, William Jennings Bryan, John Phillips Sousa, Anna Pavlova, Lillie Langtry, Oscar Wilde, Lillian Russell, Sarah Bernhardt, Al Jolson, the Marx Brothers, Tex Ritter and his horse, the Ziegfield Follies, Maude Adams, and George Burns and Gracie Allen.

When the opera house opened on January 4, 1896, the *Galveston Daily News* called it "The grandest Temple of Thespis to be found in the broad confines of Texas or the Southwest." Motion pictures were introduced during a performance of *Carmen* in 1896. "Incidental to the performance will be seen 'The Bull Fight' by the marvelous Eidoloscope," announced the *Daily News*. In 1924, A. Martini remodelled the building as a movie house and called it the Martini Theatre. In 1937, it was renamed the State. The theatre closed its doors in 1974, after which members of the Galveston County Cultural Arts Council acquired the opera house to restore it for the performing arts. Parts of the auditorium have been refurbished, while the upper stories of the Hotel Grand building have been converted to apartments. The air shaft between the buildings has been enclosed. Shops are planned for the first level of the hotel building, which is also owned by the Arts Council.

The Grand upstaged the Tremont Opera House, which opened in 1871. Prior to that, opera troupes performed at Neitsch's Theater, built in 1854.

The 1894 Grand Opera House now features a year round schedule of performing arts.

Willis-Moody House

44

WILLIS-MOODY HOUSE
1894
2618 Broadway

This 30-room mansion was built for Narcissa Worsham Willis, the widow of a rich merchant. William H. Tyndall was the architect. Tyndall, largely a designer of industrial buildings and fire stations, created a house that was modern in many ways. His architectural practice probably faltered shortly after the turn of the century, because he then joined the

U.S. Army Engineer's office in Galveston, where he was employed until his death in 1907.

Tyndall apparently did not share the Victorian penchant for embellishment. With the exception of the curved west side of the mansion, the texture of the red brick walls is uniformly flat, broken only by the limestone trim. The cornice moldings and window trim are relatively plain. While the rounded arches and massive character of the house suggest the Romanesque style, the design is much simpler than those of the Landes and Gresham houses. Each of the three towers is different in shape—round, square, octagonal—but none offers any surprises. The towers, all of the same scale and height, seem to counteract each other.

Convenience was a premium concern in Mrs. Willis's household. The ground floor basement had butler's quarters, a furnace room, a storage room for coal, a water heater for the conservatory, an elevator, a dumbwaiter, and a "clothes dryer" that circulated hot air from a stove over clothing racks. Also at ground level is a *porte cochere* with ornamental ironwork. The noted firm of Pottier & Stymus of New York designed the interiors. African mahogany, white oak, cherry, birch, and bird's-eye maple are among the fine woods used for the interior finish. The dining room is 26 feet wide by 42 feet long. The fireplace, side board, and paneling are of African mahogany, below an elaborate plaster frieze.

Mrs. Willis had married Richard Short Willis in 1847. A native of Maryland, Willis came to Texas with two brothers and opened a store at Washington on the Brazos. In 1867, after successful ventures at several other locations in Texas, he and his brother P. J. moved their wholesale dry goods and grocery business from Houston to Galveston. Willis expanded his interests to include banking, railroads, and cotton. His wife bore him 10 children. After her husband's death in 1893, Narcissa Willis razed the family home on Broadway and built the present house in its place.

Richard Fealey was the chief mason for the house. His skillful work can be seen in the Gresham House and in the State Capitol in Austin. Fealey was killed when one of the stone arches collapsed during construction of the Willis-Moody House.

Narcissa Willis died in 1899. The house escaped serious damage when the 1900 storm struck the following year. However, perhaps because of the general turmoil in the aftermath of the storm, her heirs in New York sold the house to William Lewis Moody, Jr., for $20,000. It had cost $80,000 to build.

The life of W. L. Moody, Jr., who became one of the wealthiest men in the nation, is described in the notes about the W. L. Moody Building. The Willis-Moody House is the present home of Moody's daughter, Mary Moody Northen, who was born in 1892. She is active in numerous charitable causes in Texas, including historic preservation.

45

HUTCHINGS SEALY BANK BUILDING
1895
The Strand & 24th Street

This three-story structure is actually two buildings intended to appear as one. It was designed to be a formidable house of finance for Ball, Hutchings & Company, an empire that was built by George Ball, John Hutchings, John and George Sealy, and their offspring. The corner building is 30 feet wide, while the east building is twice that.

Observers look at the red limestone of the first story and the yellow brick and terra cotta of the upper stories and assume that the building was beheaded in a storm, and that only the first story remains of the original building. This is not the case. Nicholas Clayton designed this building and there is no reason to believe that the color contrast was any different at the time of construction. Neo-Renaissance in style, the building is made of brick with stone and terra-cotta facing. Polished granite pillars flank the corner entrance to the west build-

Hutchings Sealy Bank Building

James Fadden Building

ing. Above the stone first story, brick pilasters rise to an elaborate cornice, which contains a Lone Star motif.

John Henry Hutchings was born in Raleigh, North Carolina, in 1822. He came to Texas in 1845 and worked for a Galveston dry goods house, where he met John Sealy. In 1847, the two men left the island to form their own dry goods firm at Sabine Pass. A yellow fever epidemic caused the young entrepreneurs to return to Galveston, where they joined George Ball in the firm of Ball, Hutchings & Co., a banking and merchant commission house.

Ball died in 1884 and left much of his fortune to charity. Prior to his death, he donated $50,000 for the construction of a magnificent public school, and his estate donated an equal amount for its completion. The public high school in Galveston was named for George Ball. Unfortunately, the original school building, a great domed structure designed in the spirit of a state capitol, has been demolished.

Hutchings fathered nine children and was active in city government and in the promotion of harbor improvements. He was president of the powerful Galveston Wharf Company and was also instrumental in bringing the Mallory Line to Galveston. He died in 1906.

John Sealy was born in Kingston, Pennsylvania, in 1822, the same year as Hutchings. He came to Galveston in 1846. He helped launch the Galveston Gas Company and was active in the railroad business. Sealy, who died in 1884, left part of his fortune for the construction of a hospital in Galveston for the treatment of all, without regard for citizens' ability to pay. The John Sealy Hospital is now a large medical facility affiliated with the University of Texas Medical Branch.

Another occupant of the building was John Sealy's son, John Sealy II. Born in Galveston in 1870 and a graduate of Princeton, John II took his father's considerable empire and expanded it exponentially. With partners, he acquired the Navarro Refining Company of Corsicana and the Security Oil Company of Beaumont. These firms were joined as Magnolia Petroleum, named for Sealy's aunt, Magnolia Willis Sealy. The resulting firm participated in the huge oil discoveries of East Texas. While the company maintained offices in the Hutchings Sealy Building, its headquarters were in Dallas. In 1925, Magnolia merged with the Standard Oil Company of New York.

John II was also a great supporter of the hospital system named for his father, and with his sister, Mrs. R. Waverly Smith, he established the Sealy-Smith Foundation for the benefit of the hospital.

When Texas's first bank, the Commercial and Agricultural Bank, founded by Samuel May Williams, was disbanded in 1859 by court order, Ball, Hutchings & Co. assumed its assets and liabilities. In 1879, the bank changed its name to Hutchings, Sealy & Company. After a merger in 1930, the bank became First Hutchings-Sealy National Bank, a name that would stand until it was acquired by InterFirst Corporation in 1982. By virtue of its ties with the Commercial and Agricultural Bank, the present institution lays claim to being the oldest bank in Texas.

In 1984–85, this building was renovated for use as shops, offices, and a restaurant. Though not one of architect Clayton's most vibrant designs, the

Hutchings Sealy Bank Building is still a massive and impressive structure indicative of Galveston's prosperity in the decade preceding the Great Storm of 1900.

46
JAMES FADDEN BUILDING
1898
2410-12 The Strand

Nicholas Clayton designed this small, handsome building. James Fadden and Company was a wholesale dealer of liquors, wines, and cigars. To make the two-story structure more impressive, a false half-story was added to the facade. The building has cast-iron columns on the first story, and the brickwork of the second level shows a high level of craftsmanship. The large original cornice is gone.

Isaac Heffron House

47
ISAAC HEFFRON HOUSE
1899–1900
511 17th Street

Unlike most Galveston houses, the Heffron residence has a strong horizontal emphasis, a trait that would gain wide acceptance in the 20th century. With its round porches and unusual columns, the house looks half steamboat.

Isaac Heffron, a native of Wales, was a cement contractor who built the railway trestle bridge to Galveston, the water works, and the first sewerage systems for Galveston and Houston. While the late-Victorian structure was completed shortly before the great 1900 storm ravaged the island, the home was undamaged. The Heffron family occupied the house for 43 years.

Galveston architect Charles Bulger designed the house. He built an identical residence for another client in Temple, Texas.

The Heffron House is now operated as a bed-and-breakfast hostelry called the Victorian Inn.

48
LUCAS TERRACES
1902–8
1407-9 Broadway

After the 1900 storm destroyed his apartment house on Broadway near the beach, also called the Lucas Terraces, Thomas Lucas immediately set about salvaging the wreckage for usable brick. He stored the bricks in the street near his cottage at Broadway and 14th Street, until the city ordered him to remove them. In 1902, Lucas started work on the east building of the present Terraces. The two are separate buildings joined by iron rods and the masonry center terrace, now enclosed with windows. Because Lucas could only afford to work on his project in his spare time, progress was slow. He completed the east building in 1907. To make room for the second structure, Lucas moved his own cottage. Rental income from the first building enabled him to finish the second within a year.

Lucas did most of the labor himself and reused the brick, so the apartments cost only $17,000 to build. Lucas was 77 years old when he celebrated the opening of the second building. A newspaper ac-

Lucas Terraces

count of the event reported, "The houses are strictly modern English in design and in the drawing and specifications…Mr. Lucas was his own architect."[33] It is obvious that Lucas, who was born in Nottingham, England, was no ordinary bricklayer. His creation is a handsome expression of the *art nouveau* style, with delightful shell-motif window boxes and coral-shaped railings.

Sacred Heart Church

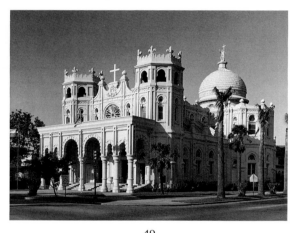

49
SACRED HEART CHURCH
1903–4
14th Street and Broadway

The magnificent Romanesque church that Nicholas Clayton designed for Sacred Heart parish was destroyed by the 1900 storm. Photographs made at the time show only two walls left standing. In spite of the fact that Clayton prepared plans for rebuilding the church, it was decided to build anew, perhaps in the interest of economy. The *Daily News* quoted the parish rector in 1903: "We shall rebuild our church of concrete. On our premises there is about $7,000 worth of debris from the old church. This we shall break up into small pieces and utilize in the concrete in putting up the main walls."[34]

The design of the new building appears to have been assigned to a Brother Jimenez, a member of the Jesuit order. The design is said to have been based on the Church of the Immaculate Conception in New Orleans, built in 1857, which was in turn modelled after Port Santa Maria, a chapel in Spain built by the Moors. The new Sacred Heart was smaller than its predecessor. The hurricane of 1915 damaged the dome of the church, and Nicholas Clayton designed a larger, more impressive replacement, which survives today. The present dome is 100 feet high.

St. Mary's University, built in 1851, was the original structure on this block. In 1884, the Jesuits assumed control of the school until they gave the complex, including the Sacred Heart Church, to the local diocese in 1923. At that time, the university was closed, and the college buildings were used for a

parochial school. Today, the brilliant white Moorish church shares the block with the rectory, built in 1925, and school buildings erected in the 1950s and 60s.[35]

Daniel W. Kempner House

50
DANIEL W. KEMPNER HOUSE
1907
2504 Avenue O

In 1906, Daniel Webster Kempner married Jeane Bertig of Paragould, Arkansas. The next year, when Kempner built this large home for his bride, he chose a style that was new to the city. Perhaps after the difficult years Galveston experienced in the wake of the 1900 storm, Kempner felt his trendy post-Victorian home might portend a better era for his family and the island. In any event, Kempner commissioned the St. Louis architectural firm of Mauran, Russell and Garden to design this Spanish Colonial mansion.

Kempner was the second son born to Eliza and Harris Kempner, who had 11 children. His father was active in the grocery business, real estate, sugar refining, and banking. After graduating from the University of Virginia in 1898, Daniel Kempner travelled widely. His dispatches from overseas were often published by the *Galveston Tribune* as a regular feature entitled "The Innocent Abroad." He later joined the family businesses and served as president of Imperial Sugar Co. and of Texas Export and Import Co. He was also involved in flour mill, cotton compress, and oil ventures.

Kempner purchased a large tract of land from the Ursuline nuns, whose convent and school are due north of his house. The property that was not used for his home was sold to friends of the Kempner family, who in turn built many of the impressive houses that now line Avenue O between 25th and 27th streets.

The Kempner House is of wood frame with a stucco exterior. The two-and-a-half story structure is crowned by mission-style gable ends and a red tile roof. Unlike most earlier Galveston buildings, the house is only slightly raised above ground level. The once-ornate front dormer was simplified in the 1960s following storm damage.

The house has remained in the family and now belongs to Daniel Kempner's sole grandson. In 1981, a pool and pool house were added. The extensive grounds include a greenhouse and many live oak and palm trees.

Kempner's departure from traditional Galveston styles was popular. For in 1910, when a group of civic leaders proposed to build a large beach hotel to reestablish the island as a tourist attraction, Kempner's St. Louis architects were hired to design a second Spanish Colonial structure, the Galvez Hotel.

51
GALVEZ HOTEL
1910–11
2024 Seawall Boulevard

A fire destroyed the spectacular Beach Hotel, designed by Nicholas Clayton, in 1898. The 1900 storm levelled everything else on or near the shore. By 1910, however, Galveston was back on its feet again. At that time, a number of business leaders felt that the construction of a luxury hotel would

help to rebuild the city's resort trade and announce to the world that Galveston had recovered from its disaster. Four local concerns subscribed $200,000 to the project and additional money was quickly raised. The firm of Mauran, Russell & Garden of St. Louis designed a six-story Spanish Colonial Revival hotel to be built on the new Seawall Boulevard.

The hotel was named after Bernardo de Galvez, for whom the city is named. The building is of stuccoed brick with mission parapets and a red tile roof. The rounded arches of the first story and the central tower and iron balconies also reflect the Spanish Colonial Revival.

The hotel was a success. *Hotel Monthly* described it in 1912 as one of the "best arranged and most richly and tastefully furnished seaside hotels in America." The hotel soon became the center of social life in Galveston. Many balls and parties were held there and numerous young women made their debuts in the Galvez ballroom. In 1937, President Franklin Roosevelt made the Galvez his headquarters while fishing the waters of the Gulf. General Douglas MacArthur and then-General Dwight D. Eisenhower were guests there. Actress Alice Fay and orchestra leader Phil Harris were married at the hotel in 1941.

Sam Maceo, the island's most powerful gambling impressario, was once a barber at the Galvez Hotel. He later lived in its penthouse.

The hotel was purchased by an investor group including Dr. Denton A. Cooley in 1978. The following year the Galvez was refurbished and several structural changes were made. An indoor swimming pool was added to the front entrance, and a wing of motel rooms, not original to the building, was removed. The hotel is now called Marriott's Hotel Galvez.

52
CITY NATIONAL BANK
1919–20
2219 Market

Near the turn of the century, the Classic Revival, which had profoundly influenced Galveston's 19th century architecture, was again "revived." When businessman W. L. Moody, Jr., decided to build a new home for his City National Bank, his architects chose the Neo-Classical style. But the Chicago firm

of Weary & Alford had several problems to confront. First, the site, flanked by two large buildings, was very narrow. Second, the owner wanted an imposing building but did not care to pay for expensive granite, the logical material for such a structure. Finally, the first floor needed to be eight feet above street level as a precaution against flooding.

Because the building was wedged between two larger neighbors, only the facade received architectural ornament. Hence when the magnificent four-story cast-iron structure to the east was razed in 1964, the bank's plain side was exposed, betraying the elaborate front. Without its neighbor, the bank's Classical facade looks like a mask worn by a homely box.

The tall pedestals supporting the building's Corinthian columns are of granite, with bas relief decoration. However, for the remaining facade, the architects substituted cheaper terra-cotta, which had been glazed to resemble granite. The granite stairway between the pedestals rises the requisite eight feet. The doors, window trim, and the huge urns between the paired columns are of bronze.[36]

The interior was more successful. It includes an impressive barrel vault ceiling with skylights. The ceiling is richly ornamented plaster, including gilded medallions and painted highlights. The front and rear mezzanines are original, while the connecting galleries are later additions. The wainscoting and pilasters are of Italian marble.

City National Bank was founded by Moody in 1907. In 1953, a year before his death, its name was changed to Moody National Bank. The building now houses the Galveston County Historical Museum.

53
SANTA FE RAILROAD BUILDING
(SHEARN MOODY PLAZA)
1931–32
25th Street and The Strand

This art deco building was erected to house the headquarters of the Gulf, Colorado & Santa Fe Railroad and the company's local passenger terminal. The terminal replaced the four-story Romanesque Santa Fe Station, which was razed to make room for its successor. An adjacent building, also owned by the railroad, was incorporated into the present structure's south wing. The building has an 11-story central tower flanked by two 8-story wings. The tower is topped by a ziggurat, the popular art deco treatment for towers inspired by Babylonian temples.

The reinforced concrete foundation of the building rests on 30-to-40-foot pilings driven into the ground. The walls, supported by a structural steel frame, are of brick with terra-cotta facing.

The Santa Fe Railroad offices were moved from Galveston in 1960, and the company considered demolishing the building in 1974. The Galveston Historical Foundation and local preservationists persuaded the company to make further attempts at selling the building. In 1976 the Moody Foundation acquired the building and spent $10 million on its rehabilitation. It was then renamed Shearn Moody Plaza, for Shearn Moody, Sr., the grandson of W. L. Moody. In 1982 the Center for Transportation and Commerce, a railroad museum developed by the Moody Foundation, opened in the restored passenger depot.[37]

For the researcher interested in Galveston's historic structures, several unpublished sources are particularly valuable. The U.S. Department of the Interior's National Register of Historic Places nomination forms contain a great deal of information. Many of the buildings illustrated in this volume have been placed on the register. The Historic American Buildings Survey, conducted in 1966 and 1969, includes history and descriptions of many structures. Similarly useful are the papers of Betty Hartman and Jane Chapin, both professional researchers in Galveston, and the programs published by the Galveston Historical Foundation in conjunction with its annual historic homes tour. All of these materials are available at the Rosenberg Library's Galveston & Texas History Center in Galveston.

[1] Ruth Evelyn Kelly, " 'Twixt Failure and Success: The Port of Galveston in the 19th Century," MS, (University of Houston, 1975), p. 4.

[2] Francis Sheridan, *Galveston Island: Or, A Few Months Off the Coast of Texas, 1839–1840,* (Austin: Univ. of Texas Press, 1954), p. 46; Earl Wesley Fornell, *The Galveston Era,* (Austin: Univ. of Texas Press, 1961), p. 5.

[3] Charles W. Hayes, *History of the Island and the City of Galveston,* written in 1879, (Austin: Jenkins Garrett Press, 1974), II, pp. 699–700.

[4] John Maass, *The Gingerbread Age,* (New York: Rinehart & Co., 1957), p. 53.

[5] Fornell, pp. 90–2.

[6] Sheridan, p. 46; Fornell, p. 8.

[7] Bernard Marinbach, *Galveston: Ellis Island of the West,* (Albany: State Univ. of New York Press, 1983).

[8] Sheridan, p. 45.

[9] Fornell, p. 5.

[10] Drury Blakeley Alexander, *Texas Homes of the 19th Century,* (Austin: Univ. of Texas Press, 1966), p. 85.

[11] Maass, p. 97.

[12] Ibid, p. 64.

[13] Mary Jane Riddle Menard, letter to James Clemens, Jr., Mary Clemens Collection, (St. Louis University, 1844).

[14] Virginia Eisenhour, *Galveston: A Different Place,* (Galveston: V. Eisenhour, 1983), p. 34.

[15] Margaret Swett Henson, *Samuel May Williams, Early Texas Entrepreneur,* (College Station: Texas A&M Univ. Press, 1976), passim.

[16] Hayes, p. 468.

[17] *Galveston Daily News,* September 6, 1908, p. 5.

[18] Betty Hartman, "The Hendley Row," MS, Hartman Papers, (Galveston: Rosenberg Library, n.d.), p. 2.

[19] Hayes, p. 870.

[20] Rifkind, Carole, *A Field Guide to American Architecture,* (New York: New American Library, 1980), p. 63.

[21] Howard Barnstone, *The Galveston That Was,* (New York: Macmillan Publishing Co., 1966), pp. 36–43; Fornell, p. 293.

[22] *Flake's Daily Bulletin,* December 5, 1869, p. 1.

[23] William A. Ward, "The League-Blum Building," MS, (Austin: Texas Historical Commission, n.d.), p. 3.

[24] Maass, p. 55.

[25] Galveston Historical Foundation, 1983 *Annual Historical Homes Tour* program, (Galveston: 1983), pp. 18–21.

[26] Fornell, p. 33.

[27] Betty Hartman, "The Leon & H. Blum Building," MS, Hartman Papers, (Galveston: Rosenberg Library, n.d.), pp. 3–6.

[28] Andrew Morrison, *Industries of Galveston,* (Metropolitan Publishing Co., 1887), p. 77.

[29] Tom Alpert & Bonnie Powers, "The Kauffman-Runge Stewart Title Building," MS, (Austin: Texas Historical Commission, n.d.), pp. 1–3.

[30] John Garner, project supervisor, Historic American Buildings Survey, (Washington: Library of Congress, 1966–67).

[31] Barnstone, p. 122.

[32] *History of Texas,* (Chicago: Lewis Publishing Co., 1895), pp. 650–51.

[33] *Galveston Daily News,* May 17, 1908, p. 18.

[34] *Galveston Daily News,* January 9, 1903, p. 10.

[35] Betty Hartman, "The Sacred Heart Church," MS, (Galveston: Rosenberg Library n.d.), pp. 2–10.

[36] I. T. Frary, "City National Bank of Galveston," *Architectural Record,* February, 1921, pp. 186–87.

[37] *Shipper's Digest,* May 25, 1932, pp. 3–9; *Galveston Daily News,* December 9, 1962, p. 6B; Gianni Longo, Jean Tatge, and Lois Fishman, eds., *Learning From Galveston,* (New York: Institute for Environmental Action, 1983), p. 83.

Alexander, Drury Blakeley. *Texas Homes of the 19th Century*. Austin: University of Texas Press, 1966.

Alpert, Tom, and Bonnie Powers. "The Kauffman-Runge Stewart Title Building." MS. Austin: Texas Historical Commission, n.d.

Barnstone, Howard. *The Galveston That Was*. New York: Macmillan Publishing Co., 1966.

Chapin, Jane. "Mallory or Produce Building." MS. Austin: Texas Historical Commission, 1984.

Eisenhour, Virginia. *Galveston: A Different Place*. Galveston: V. Eisenhour, 1983.

Eisenhour, Virginia. *The Strand of Galveston*. Galveston: V. Eisenhour, 1973.

Fornell, Earl Wesley. *The Galveston Era*. Austin: University of Texas Press, 1961.

Garner, John. Historic American Buildings Survey. Washington: Library of Congress, 1966–67.

Gustafson, Eleanor H. "The Open Gates: The George Sealy House in Galveston." *Antiques*, September, 1975, pp. 508–14, (Reprinted by Harris County Heritage Society, Houston).

Hartman, Betty. Hartman Papers. Galveston: Rosenberg Library.

Hayes, Charles W. *History of the Island and the City of Galveston*. 2 vols. (Written in 1879). Austin: Jenkins Garrett Press, 1974.

Henson, Margaret Swett. *Samuel May Williams: Early Texas Entrepreneur*. College Station: Texas A&M Univ. Press, 1976.

Kelly, Ruth Evelyn. " 'Twixt Failure and Success: The Port of Galveston in the 19th Century," MS. Houston: University of Houston, 1975.

Lester, Paul. *The Great Galveston Disaster*. Philadelphia: International Publishing, 1900.

Longo, Gianni, Jean Tatge, and Lois Fishman, eds. *Learning From Galveston*. New York: Institute for Environmental Action, 1983.

Maass, John. *The Gingerbread Age*. New York: Rinehart & Co., 1957.

Marinbach, Bernard. *Galveston: Ellis Island of the West*. Albany: State Univ. of New York Press, 1983.

Miller, Ray. *Ray Miller's Galveston*. Houston: Cordovan Press, 1983.

Morrison, Andrew. *Industries of Galveston*. n.p., Metropolitan Publishing, 1887.

National Register of Historic Places, Galveston nomination forms. Washington: Library of Congress.

Rifkind, Carole. *A Field Guide to American Architecture*. New York: New American Library, 1980.

ERA OF FOREIGN FLAGS

1520s

Karankawa Indians fished and hunted on the barrier island.

1528

Shipwrecked on the island, Cabeza de Vaca and three companions are believed to have been held captive by the Karankawas.

1685

Robert Cavalier, Sieur de La Salle, the French explorer, sailed into Matagorda Bay, mistaking it for the mouth of the Mississippi River. Although La Salle never landed on the island, he claimed it for France and named it Saint Louis, after his king, Louis XIV.

1690

The island came under the Spanish flag.

1783

Spanish surveyors christened the island in honor of the governor of Louisiana, Bernardo de Galvez.

1816

Louis-Michel Aury named himself civil and military governor of Texas and the island.

1817

Pirate Jean Laffite arrived on the island from New Orleans and established a town called Campeachy.

1820

The island's population was 1,000.

1821

The activities of Laffite and his men brought them into disfavor with the U.S. Government. After receiving orders to abandon the island, he set fire to his own town and sailed away. The Mexican flag flew over Galveston.

1825

Stephen F. Austin secured the legalization of a port at Galveston.

1830

A custom house was built by the Mexican Government, and the first attempts were made to collect taxes. The island's population was 500.

ERA OF THE REPUBLIC OF TEXAS AND EARLY STATEHOOD

1836

Texas won its independence from Mexico. News of the victory was received by the provisional president of the Republic of Texas, David Burnett, and his cabinet while they were on the island. Galveston became the temporary capital of Texas. Colonel Michel B. Menard's land purchase was confirmed by the Republic. Menard and his partners later formed the Galveston City Co. (1839), and proceeded to lay out the town and offer lots for sale. John Grosbeck was contracted to make a survey and map of the city.

1837

Galveston was made a port of entry by the congress of the Republic. A hurricane devastated the island. A post office was established.

1838

General Sam Houston was elected the first president of the Republic of Texas. Galveston was made a county seat. A ferry was established between the Texas mainland and the island, whose population was approximately 3,000. Texas's first bakery opened on the island.

1839

Galveston received its city charter. The first mayor, J.M. Allen, was elected.

1840

Samuel May Williams, Stephen F. Austin, and Thomas McKinney, completed the first wharf. Shipping was increasing with European countries. An act was passed by the Texas congress providing that mail should be carried between Houston and Galveston. The First Presbyterian Church was organized.

1841

Galveston Artillery Co. was chartered.

1842

The *Galveston Daily News,* the oldest newspaper in Texas, was established under the banner of the *Galveston News*.

1843

The first ship carrying German immigrants arrived in Galveston.

1845

Texas was admitted to the Union. Galveston was the largest city, with a population of approximately 5,000. Acts of Congress called for the erection of a lighthouse and the establishment of a hospital on the island.

1846

John Sealy and John H. Hutchings met in Galveston and became business partners. The first Federal court in Galveston was formed, with John Charles Watrous being named Federal judge by President Polk. St. Mary's Cathedral was dedicated.

1848

The first incorporated bank in Texas, the Commercial and Agricultural Bank of Galveston, was founded.

1854

The Galveston Wharf Co. was organized.

1860

The Galveston, Houston and Henderson Railroad bridge connected Galveston to the mainland. The island's population was 9,000.

1861

Sam Houston, who had lobbied hard for the admission of Texas to the Union, came to Galveston and spoke strongly against secession. Despite his efforts, Texans voted by a margin of 4–1 to secede.

1862

The Port of Galveston was closed by the Federal blockade, forcing businesses such as Hutchings, Sealy & Co. and the *Daily News* to move to Houston. Federal forces occupied the island.

1863

Confederate General John B. Magruder made preparations to recapture Galveston. The ensuing Battle of Galveston was won by the Confederates, who thereafter controlled the city until the end of the Civil War.

ERA OF WEALTH AND INFLUENCE

1865

Galveston surrendered to Federal authorities. Slaves in Texas were emancipated on June 19. The First National Bank of Galveston, the first bank to operate in Texas under the National Bank Act of 1863, was founded.

1866

Colonel William Lewis Moody arrived on the island from Fairfield, Texas, The *Daily News* and many other businesses that had departed during the Civil War returned to Galveston. St. Mary's Orphanage, the first orphanage in Texas, was organized. The first streetcar franchise in Galveston was granted.

1867

The first Galveston Mardi Gras was held.

1868

Of the 15 private banks in Texas, 7 had their addresses in Galveston.

1869

The City of Houston began dredging Buffalo Bayou.

1870

Five years after the abolition of slavery, the Shiloh African Methodist Episcopal Church (A.M.E.) was founded. Harris Kempner moved to Galveston from Cold Springs. The population of Galveston was 13,818.

1871

The Galveston Historical Society was founded. A National Weather Service office, the first in Texas and among the first 15 in the U.S., was established in Galveston.

1872

Nicholas J. Clayton, destined to become the most prominent architect in Galveston, arrived on the island. The first Galveston Cotton Exchange opened.

1873

In May, the Texas legislature passed an act chartering the Gulf, Colorado and Santa Fe Railway Co., with its headquarters in Galveston.

1877

Clarke & Courts brought the first lithograph press to Texas for printing from stone. It was installed in their plant on the island.

1878

The first telephone in Galveston was installed for Colonel A.H. Belo, in the Galveston Daily News Building.

1880

Former President Ulysses S. Grant visited Galveston for a banquet at the Tremont Hotel. The island's population was 22,248.

1881

Texans voted to place the state medical college in Galveston.

1882

Electricity was brought to Galveston. Ball High School was built.

1883

Long distance telephone service began between Galveston and Houston.

1885

Central High School, the first black high school in Texas, was opened in Galveston.

1889

An agreement was reached with the U.S. Government to develop a deep-water port at Galveston.

1890

The city was granted authority for the operation of its first electric streetcar. A year later, the streetcar was in operation. Texas's first medical college building (Old Red) was opened in Galveston. John Sealy Hospital and the first training school for nurses also opened. Galveston's population was 29,084.

1891

President Benjamin Harrison visited.

1893

A wagon bridge across Galveston Bay was completed.

1894

The Grand Opera House opened.

1896

A great snow spread 15.4 inches on the unsuspecting island. Galveston became a deep-sea world port with the completion of the Galveston Harbor jetties system. The channel's draft was 25 feet.

1898

Galveston boasted the first golf course and the first country club in Texas.

ERA OF THE GREAT STORM AND RECOVERY

1900

The most destructive hurricane in U.S. history hit Galveston, resulting in the death of 6,000 people and the destruction of 3,600 structures. Galvestonians went to work rebuilding. The island's population was 37,788.

1901

The commission form of city government, first in the nation, was established in Galveston to address problems resulting from the 1900 storm. The age of petroleum began with the gusher at Spindletop.

1902

For protection from future storms, construction began on a seawall. Grade raising also began on the island.

1904

The first section of the seawall was completed. The Rosenberg Library opened.

1910

Galveston's population was 36,981.

1911

The Galvez Hotel opened.

1912

The Galveston Causeway opened. Interurban trains began running between Galveston and Houston.

1915

Another serious storm hit the city. This did far less damage because of the seawall and the grade raising.

ERA OF THE "OPEN CITY"

1922

Galveston's "Open City" era began. Gambling establishments and bordellos were booming businesses on the island.

1928

The new Mambo Line steamship, *Algonquin,* arrived on its first trip between New York and Galveston. A contract was awarded to the Orleans Dredging Co. to dredge Galveston channel.

1929

Galveston was the second largest export port in the U.S. Air passenger service connected Galveston, Houston, Waco, Dallas, and Fort Worth. Dredging on Bolivar Ferry landing began.

1930

Galveston's population was 52,938.

1932

The Galveston Municipal Airport opened.

1934

The world's first streamliner train, the Rock Island Rocket, visited Galveston.

1935

Three paid lifeguards formed the first beach patrol in the history of Galveston.

1937

President Franklin D. Roosevelt visited Galveston, where he met Congressman Lyndon B. Johnson. The President used the Galvez Hotel as a temporary White House.

1940

The island's population was 60,862.

1941

An Army airbase opened on Galveston Island.

1942

The Pleasure Pier at the foot of 25th Street was completed. Made of concrete, it extended 1,600 feet into the Gulf of Mexico.

1943–1945

A World War II prisoner-of-war camp was located on the island.

1951

The "Little Kefauver" hearings in Austin investigated Galveston's gambling and prostitution.

1957

The "Open City" era ended. Will Wilson, attorney general of Texas, is credited with closing down the island's many casinos and bars.

ERA OF THE RENAISSANCE

1961

Hurricane Carla hit Galveston. Tornadoes that came in its aftermath caused severe damage. A council/manager form of government was adopted by the city.

1962

Galveston was selected as the site for the first Shriners' Burn Institute. An extension of Galveston's seawall was completed. The entire length is now 10.4 miles.

1966

Under the supervision of the Galveston Historical Foundation, Galveston's 19th-century architectural structures were documented by the Historic American Building Survey.

1969

The Junior League of Galveston County undertook restoration of the 1881 Trueheart-Adriance Building. The song "Galveston," written by Jim Webb and recorded by Glen Campbell, was presented to the city council to be Galveston's official song.

1970

The island's population was 61,809. The Strand area was listed on the National Register of Historic Places.

1971

The East End Historical District became a locally protected historic district. Five years later, the East End and The Strand would become National Historic Landmark Districts. Galveston's tallest building, the 20-story American National Insurance Company Tower, was completed.

1973

A revolving fund was set up by The Moody Foundation and the Kempner Fund to revitalize The Strand. The Galveston Historical Foundation hired its first executive director. The first annual "Dickens's Evening on The Strand," now a tradition of the Galveston Historical Foundation, was held.

1974

The restored Ashton Villa opened after years of preparation.

1975

Galveston's Silk Stocking Historic District, a local historic district, was established.

1980

Galveston's population was 61,902.

1982

The Center for Transportation and Commerce (Railroad Museum) opened. The Galveston Historical Foundation completed restoration of the *Elissa,* an iron barque built in 1877, as an operational sailing ship and a maritime museum at Pier 21, near The Strand.

1983

Hurricane Alicia hit Galveston. Losses totalled approximately $500 million.

1984

The city council voted to accept $10.7 million in grants and private local contributions to fund a proposed four-mile trolley system. On April 23, *USA Today* listed Galveston among the most desirable 25 U.S. cities in which to live. Galveston was being called "boomtown," and renewal and restoration were visible in commercial and residential neighborhoods. A tax reinvestment zone, the city's 10th, was created to stimulate growth and to fund public improvements in the downtown area. The restored 1839 Samuel May Williams Home opened in March. England's Princess Anne visited in January.

1985

The final phase of restoration of the 1894 Grand Opera House began.

1985

Galveston's tradition of Mardi Gras, which began in 1867, was revived with a grand night parade attracting over 200,000 to the island. The celebration was held in conjunction with the opening of the Tremont House, a landmark restoration hotel in The Strand district.

—Mary Remmers